Dear El[...]

Thank you!

GETTING TO THE HEARTS OF TEACHING

HUMANITIES, EDUCATION, ARTS, REFLECTION,
TECHNOLOGY AND SCIENCE FOR A
COLLABORATIVE CLASSROOM

CASEY JAKUBOWSKI, PHD

Casey

ISBN: 978-1-959347-26-2

CONTENTS

INTRODUCTION OR WHERE DID WE GO WRONG?

When I was a child, I wanted to be an archaeologist, or an Egyptologist. I also wanted to be a firefighter, a navy officer, and later, a starship captain. I loved science museums, I loved history. I loved doing experiments with my chemist father, and learning CPR with my mom, a nurse. Later I wanted to study cardiology or thoracic surgery, especially when my little brother Adam was sick in the hospital. My desire to wander among science, technology, history, geography, medicine, and service is not uncommon for many children in schools.

Yet today, as I write this paragraph, our students don't see the connections among the different areas of learning. And, since 2016, and with greater clarity recently, we have seen Americans who engage in conspiracy theories, dismiss science, and do not understand the basics of civics (Delisle, 2021). Americans, though highly educated, and graduates of high school at historic rates, are failing basic tests of a civilization, society, and participation. Where did we, as educators, go wrong? I posit two theories:

First, we have fetishedized disciplines. In so many places in academics, and in schools K-12, hard and fast lines exist among different disciplines, yet knowledge does not stop at boundaries. At the seventh through twelfth grade, teachers are grouped by subject matter. In colleges, departments and schools are assigned a discipline. Innovation and insight exist where disciplines collide and form new thought patterns. A hard and fast division in disciplines separates good ideas and people.

Second, we have stopped talking about real matters with children. In education, we like silos. Silos, which portray an image of separateness, also convey containment. Like old school academics, we have created disciplines that seek to separate and isolate content into neat packages (Nichols, 2017). Many teachers want to silo academics for ease. Integration in schooling is tough. It takes effort. It requires skills that go beyond what many of us have experienced in schooling. The introduction of high stakes exams into education have not helped. Students and teachers are held "accountable" for learning specific skills and content pegged into isolated disciplines. In many colleges, there are academic departments that are discipline specific. There are limited attempts at interdisciplinary work due to stresses, strains, and systems, and structures who want isolation practices.

For many educators out there, you may be saying to yourself, "but I do integrate, I collaborate!" Yes, you might, especially if you're gifted, or teach elementary school! But do you really integrate your curriculum? I want to help you try. This book will help educators, administrators, college professors, and parents look into ways to effortlessly combine the sciences, technology, engineering, math, and humanities. It's not hard. We are almost there in many ways. We just have to think for a minute strategically about what is already done in schools and examine better ways to reorganize the day and the classes to drive our students back to the child-like state of firefighter on Monday and Egyptologist on Friday.

Reflecting on Why

As I have engaged in a twenty-year career in education, I traveled to urban, suburban, and rural districts (Jakubowski, 2021). I have seen students in some of the poorest academically performing districts engaged and learning and excited about knowledge. I have seen students in some of our strongest performing districts who are utterly bored and disengaged. The students are doing very well on standardized tests and pre-determined factoid assessments. But our students are not experiencing learning in *context*. It's not their fault. It is most certainly not the teacher's fault. It's a systemic fault. School was designed to warehouse students daily to keep them from the labor force. Larry Cuban and David Tyack are two eminent scholars of education history who have written on the subject (Tyack & Cuban, 1995). Today, school is designed as a sorting mechanism for the workforce. There is some sociology behind that, and if you are interested, Jennifer Ballantine, et al., (2018) has done a great job approaching the system. The way we measure schools, as written about by a number of educational and social scientists including leading researchers in the field, including Campbell Scribner, Jason Cervone, Kai Schafft, Jack Schneider, Catherine Biddle, Amy Anzano, Erin McHenry Sorber, and Daniella Sutherland, creates a massive deficit narrative which the government foists on the unsuspecting people. Jason Cervone (2017) describes this neo-liberal attempt to privatize schools as one of the greatest catastrophes facing education and civilization today. Without recapturing the major goal of civic education, to teach and to introduce all children to a wide range of knowledge, then we vote to cut funding and destroy our education system. Why? Because it bored us!

Reflecting on Testing

A second reason why we need to talk about reforming education has been the total silo-created schooling in the US. We must return to integrating STEM or STEAM with humanities (let's just call it HEARTS) because we are facing a disaster civically, culturally, and in the world. Our test results should not matter when our nation is literally divided. PISA and other tests show the US consistently in the middle of the pack on testing (Gjicali & Lipnevich, 2021). There has been a large amount of research conducted on why US citizens do not do well in science and math. Feel free to read any of the research reports on the topic. I once worked at a research institute that produces some of the finest scientists and engineers in the world. They are smart. They are amazing; they are driven. And they have a real difficulty thinking through science and engineering design issues. One of the classes I teach is an introduction to the design process. We as instructors struggle to get the students to identify a problem. What can they do as an engineer to fix an issue which affects society? They are smart with equations and solving assigned problems, but their creativity needs a boost. A couple of my students told me that they really never get a chance to see how science and engineering ever interacts with the arts or humanities.

A friend of mine, a trained science teacher, once said (and I am paraphrasing him) that science and engineering are the products of the culture in which they were born. Let us take a moment and ponder that thought: Science and engineering are the products of the culture in which they are born. What does culture mean? To a specialist, culture is defined as the societal practices that a group of people use in order to identify themselves, and *pass along to their children in a formalized fashion.* Culture can include:

- Religion
- Language
- Art
- Music
- Dress

- Food
- Drink
- Social norms and values (Ballentine, et al., 2017).

As you can see, it's quite a list. And often, a society will create a culture based upon the environment in which it is living. But humans aren't static. They move, they create, they invent. People have an idea, and somehow, society changes, slightly or dramatically. In social studies, we often talk about how technology is used by a group to influence the environment in which they live. It's in the National Council for Social Studies standards. It's in almost every state's set of standards. More importantly, it's an example of HEARTS integration!

Losing Mentoring

Now that I have hopefully established the values of the so-called humanities, let's turn to my second theory: We do not talk about important areas enough anymore. Where did this start? It is my firm belief that two areas destroyed our culture. Far too long people have said "children should be seen and not heard" and second, "never talk about politics, religion or money." These two phrases have created a really big problem in the US. First, children, who are very inquisitive, have for many years been shuttered out of "adult conversations" (Wells et al., 2017). Children at home, school, and in society are frequently admonished "it's none of your business." Yet HOW can a child learn? With the introduction of technology, many exhausted parents have handed a child a smart device to distract them even further from the world. I don't blame the exhausted parents. The economic demands on parents have become overwhelming (Benjamin & Komlos, 2021). Without adequate time in the day, week, month, year, or career, what is being asked of parents is astronomical.

Yet we must have conversations with children. They need mentoring. But they also need unstructured time. And contrary to what developmental psychologists have written, most Americans have over scheduled and over protected children. They need engagement and involvement in play: unstructured play, exploration, and discovery. Exploring neighborhoods and surrounding areas was always part of the older generation's experiences of growing up. Books and articles and videos and vlogs and blogs have erupted exuding the need to allow children to return to the exploration and discovery of the past. By de-scheduling children from activities, the line between school and not school may help reverse trends of children over scheduled, exhausted, and like their parents, disengaged (Jans, 2004).

Polite Conversation Points

My second point, talking about politics, religion, and money, is a really challenging area. I have heard folks, especially in America, say to never talk about the BIG THREE of politics, religion, and money, especially in polite company. My question is why? How can students/children/adults learn if they are not engaged in conversations around the foundations of society? How can we, as a society, and most importantly educators, not talk about politics, religion, and money?

Teachers in school are loath to talk about politics. In the classroom, teachers are afraid of the consequences of political discussions. Teachers have lost their jobs when their personal lives and opinions enter the classroom. The court system, public opinion, and school administration who are afraid of the ramifications of teacher activism are quick to discipline teachers who talk politics in the classroom. In fact, there have been court rulings which explicitly state that any public employee cannot use their position to promote their political view in a classroom because students are a "captive audience" (Ho et al., 2017). So a question— students are naturally curious and will ask one of the only consistent adults in their life about their political views and their beliefs. Teachers are very leery of sharing, due to the "public" lives that they lead, especially when personal views do not align with community views. As a personal example, I taught in a rural area which leaned conservative (Jakubowski, 2020). I was not conservative, nor was I egregiously liberal. Yet I had to be very careful, as a social studies teacher, to try and just teach the process of voting. I had to try and stay very close to the "just the facts" and not talk about my own personal opinion. We were advised to not wear buttons or clothing that portrayed our feelings, especially without tenure protection. As educators, when we are not allowed to talk about politics, we cannot help our students understand the *connections* to the esoteric academic curriculum. Reality for students is concrete, so report the developmental psychologists. This leads me to point two, religion as the second "rail" of danger for teachers.

Using the subway metaphor, a "third rail" is dangerous, as the third rail on a subway line contains the power and touching it will result in death. Religion is a rail. For the purpose of my arguments in this work, I do not ascribe to religion as a set of specifics. Rather, I want to discuss the values systems that are often founded in philosophy, religion, and behavioral self-regulation. As Charles Dickens (2004 version of 1843) wrote in *A Christmas Carol*, Scrooge needed the three ghosts to show him the error of his ways. In the past, the fear for one's immortal soul, out of religion, encouraged good, charitable acts and behavior. In absolutes, religion teaches a set of behaviors, rituals, and practices, with the idea that the follower, performing these rites, will be rewarded. In almost all religions or philosophy, individuals are instructed to, at the least, not hurt others. The nuances, and the depth of works by others, is getting very short shrift here. I recognize and own it, but for the benefit of my argument, when people discuss religion, often it is to interpret the basic idea of being good, doing good, and acting with benevolence to others. As a society, with people no longer discussing the religious aspect of life, we have created a group of people and generations who have embraced the idea of looking out for the self. In the 1980s, a series of movies, television programs, and other forms of popular media witnessed a massive narrative which accused "do gooders" of the 1960s and 1970s as failed. Reformers who wanted to make institutions and the government more open, more inclusive, more responsive were derided as "goody two shoes." Self-motivation, self- heroization, and the self-made were glorified, almost like the Horatio Elgar stories of the past. The 1980s witnessed in politics and media a sharp turn away from empathy and community minded support to militaristic demands for accountability, law, order, and compliance. Narratives emerged that poverty was due to someone's faults, and not systematic problems in the structure of opportunity, government, and tax laws.

Americans began to really isolate themselves by income, by ethnicity, and by other markers of difference. Duncan and Murnaine (2011), two Stanford trained experts, wrote how the wealthy retreated away from public schools and mixed neighborhoods. Reform-minded folks heard over and over that public schools were no longer the solution to, but rather the cause of problems in society. As Scribner (2016) wrote, the hypothesis of local control became a "dog whistle" to folks who wanted to defund public education as a way to punish teacher unions for their advocacy of societal change. A dog whistle is a phrase used as coded language designed to activate rage among a specific population group.

Narratives also emerged in especially rural areas and conservative suburbs that the unions, one the protectors of middle-class jobs, opportunities, and economic advancement, were actually the hindrance to reforms and improvements. Cramer (2016), Mc-Henry Sorber (2014), and I (Jakubowski, 2019) found that in many rural areas, people liked their teachers, just hated, and despised the teacher unions. Pundits called for de-unionization, and blamed unions for the fall in the late 1980s and early 1990s of many industries that decamped to overseas markets to maximize profits, limit employee wages, benefits, and safety, as well as limit the company's exposure to expensive lawsuits for destroying the environment (Moe, 2011). In sum, the time from the 1980s to the 2000s revealed an economic system which once guaranteed economic growth and security shrank, and millions of workers were tossed out.

In the 2010s, America saw the rise of "gig economy workers" who were basically freelance people hired by companies. Temporary workers became more common, and wages fell, benefits were lost, and the working adults needed two, three, and sometimes four "jobs" to ensure basic safety. As the economy shifted into the "gig" era, and teacher wages remained stagnant, the profession suffered its first real loss—potential teachers moved into more lucrative industries and left the education profession for greener pastures. This shift, to more respected professional fields, sums up what Labaree (1996) called "the trouble with ed schools" and what Rousmanire (2013) described as the "disabling history" of American educators. This leads me now to point three: money and why it's considered no longer polite to talk about it.

Santa Doesn't Bring iPads

With the fact that economic existence has become precarious since the pandemic, and with the rise of the gig economy, fewer Americans have economic stability. Families are living from credit cards to mortgage payments, a hand-to-mouth existence. With soaring college debt, credit card debt, and general downward economic progress since the 1980s, a discussion emerged online. With the mythos of Santa Claus, parents advocated for others to tell children that they bought expensive gifts, and minor gifts were from the mythical bringer of gifts. Why? So that others who did not receive the hoped for iPad or "luxury item" would not believe that they had been naughty. So, in the wealthiest country in the world, we are now changing our century old mythos to support continued economic inequality.

A second place this inequality exists is in the separation of wealth from working and poor. More often, the wealthy live in places isolated from their working, middle, and poor neighbors (Duncan & Murnaine, 2011). In times past, parents told their children to not worry about bills, income, and expenses. People do not want to talk about salary and benefits. Why? First and foremost, money is an embarrassment in the US. With wealth had come responsibility to engage in public, non-remunerated services. Second, people were embarrassed because of the need for some modicum of privacy. With increasing regularity, anti-tax groups pushed for and obtained the public salaries, benefits, contracts, and even addresses of public officials.

The desire to keep compensation packages in public space was used as a way to expand friction between people who lived in economically depressed areas and the local public servants who worked on behalf of the same people. The conservative movement used the information to call out highly trained professionals and public service as wasteful in their eyes, and create hostility between neighbors, especially as well paying jobs were stripped, sent abroad, and entire communities were decimated by economic decline and de-investment. Kathy Cramer (2016) , Erin McHenry Sorber (2014), and others have examined this putrid hatred between unions and the conservative movement pushing for the lowest tax rates possible. Billions of lobbying dollars have gone into the collective efforts to divide the American working and middle class and shift wealth to the top 1%.

Accountability

Deeply divided economically, socially, and politically, American people also began to believe narratives designed to denigrate liberal arts and humanities. Over the past 30 years, politicians, think tank managers, and even college and university leadership have publicly reduced, closed, or phased out many of the liberal arts and humanities. For many in management positions, a desire to show direct skill connections to the workforce drove these decisions. STEM and Economics/ Business alumni gave money to colleges, replacing the decreased government funding, and offsetting rising tuition dependency. A narrative emerged that the United States education system, failing students in *A Nation at Risk*, *was* now failing by not producing enough STEM graduates (Borek, 2008). Higher education and public education turned to the concept of "college and career readiness" as the ultimate measuring stick for worth, with two areas the most critical: math and communication skills. Under the 2001 No Child Left Behind, and followed by other reforms in the twenty years following, schools from K-12 were now accountable to the federal and state governments to produce students who had mastered exams in English communications and math (Jakubowski, 2021). If the schools were doing well, then no penalties were incurred. However, most "doing well schools" did not face the fiscal, demographic, or socioeconomic fractures that the poor urban schools faced. Performance tests demonstrated a truth known to researchers for generations: poverty resulted in poor test performance (Jakubowski, 2021).

The penalties for failing school wide on the tests were significant. And the federal government wanted to ensure the schools measured all groups. This included poor students, underrepresented populations, and special education students. A miss in any subgroup resulted in a finding of "in need of improvement." With different levels. First, a school in need of improvement needs to offer the opportunity for any member of the student body to transfer to a school within the district to one in good standing. And the student's federal money went with them. In the second year, the school must offer "tutoring" through verified vendors. Federal money needed to pay for students tutoring. This often resulted in one out of five federal dollars going to ineffective practices. This money, designed in the 1970s to give poor schools reading and math teachers, was now diverted into for profit tutoring companies

Introduction or Where Did We Go Wrong?

and bussing. If the test failures continued, then a school was in corrective action, and the principal was to be removed, or the used curriculum was tossed out and a new one was implemented. After another year or so, a school was then designated as "restructuring" and then 50% and more of the staff needed to be replaced, and the school must be phased out (Jakubowski, 2021).

The results of many of these federal mandates was confusion, anger, and wasted money, as larger urban schools were broken up into smaller schools. Money was spent on training teachers, many of whom were pinballed around districts based upon significant fiscal issues and pressure to appear to meet the "restructuring requirements." Administrations of superintendents, principals, and others found their budgets squeezed, and astronomical amounts of federal aid, desperately needed to overcome poverty, flowing into private companies. Charter schools opened and closed as urban districts found parents demanding new placement for their children. Many public charters would not accept children with special needs and would suspend or expel students back to public school with little provocation. These charter schools were run by large businesses and utilized militaristic and police based policies demanding compliance over real learning.

Then in the waning days of the second Bush administration, 2008 saw an economic downturn referred to as the Great Recession (Sipple & Yao, 2015). Public funding nosedived. The economy reeled. As part of the bailout of public schools, the incoming Obama administration established the Every Student Succeeds Act (ESSA) which contained three prongs: new national curriculum, new accountability, and individual teacher evaluations. Funding dried up, and instead of sending aid, the federal government placed a number of strings on much needed money (Darling-Hammond et al., 2016).

The federal government insisted that states in order to receive multi-million dollar packages of aid called "Race To The Top" adopt the

Common Core State Learning Standards. Those federally developed standards doubled down on the centrality of literacy and math, while pushing humanities, civics, and innovative fields off to the side (Darling-Hammond et al., 2016). One such debacle was the way in which New York rolled out the CCLS and utilized "textual analysis" of the Gettysburg Address as the premier example. Not inviting historians, sociologists, or scholars of social studies into the realm, a group of "Regents Fellows" mostly from English and literacy backgrounds created and delivered lessons on how to textually analyze speeches and documents without ever once discussing the context of the document (Jakubowski, 2021). Thankfully this disaster was mediated by the work of the Stanford History Education Group (Gerwin, 2014) and the C3 Social Studies teachers in developing CCLS aligned standards which emphasized the context and motivations for the documents (Swan, et al., 2012). The damage was done, as an almost generation of students were not taught how to do more historical and humanities thinking. This is unconscionable, and with the continued demand for STEM and fiscally lucrative disciplines receiving focus, I began wondering if I was even relevant. What I learned in my career as a teacher of innovation, ethics, and leadership development embedded in a top tier STEM institute teaching undergraduates the engineering design process was an amazing fact: Yes, and now more than ever I was relevant.

This book emerged out of a clear need to teach and re-integrate the HEARTS world. We not only need to use Science, Technology, Engineering, Art, Humanities, and Math, but we must as educators be strategic and explicit. We need to reflect, as practitioners and as citizens. We must scaffold the work. HEARTSing ahead will be the only way that we rebound the American creative mind, the economics of innovation, and keep the value of the humanities, human rights, and equality at the forefront.

Testing Overwhelming Learning

A critical reason this book is so desperately needed is our national obsession with TESTING and TRACKING! Growing up in New York State, I was kind of used to testing in schools. We took math tests in third grade. We took science tests yearly. In middle school we had finals every year. In high school, we had Regents Exams, which were designed as end of course evaluations to see if we knew the material, and if we did not pass the Regents Exams, then we sat for a Regents Competency Exam, also high school exams (Jakubowski, 2020). I took the SATs in order to gain admission into college. I did not realize until much later that as part of my privilege as middle class, I was exposed to testing as a way to separate me out from classmates and other school students. The tests were all part of a TRACKING mechanism that my high school used to separate out the REALLY SMART kids from the SMART kids from the AVERAGE kids, from the BELOW AVERAGE from the SPECIAL EDUCATION kids. YIKES! When I read Oakes's (2005) book on the subject, I was blown away at how rich of a curriculum I was exposed to versus what other children were exposed to. I guess I had a bit of inkling when one of my friends told me about a basic science class that he attended when I was in Regents Science class. We measured using triple beam balances for one lab, and then went on to do and learn other science-y type things, like burn corks to figure out how much heat energy it produced. My buddy spent *two whole weeks* measuring different things on a triple balance beam. And my friend loved *STAR Trek*, and could name the scientific names for the nine species that tribbles came in contact with and had a telescope to stargaze *for fun*. WTH, as kids these days would say. I also later found out many of those advanced students were then placed in Advanced Placement classes and received <u>a whole semester worth of college credits</u> by the time they graduated from high school. Testing and tracking have destroyed a number of generations' abilities to think and see patterns and interactions and connections. Rather, the students have become quite good at:

1. Answering short answers
2. Finding and answering multiple choice questions
3. Writing prompts which do not often require deep inquiry
4. Learning anything outside of the standards-based curriculum.

The answer is of course, all of the above, but that really wasn't an option on this test! I believe that HEARTS integration will allow teachers to get their students to that mythical place of deep thinking and integration that all teachers crave in the classroom. This is project based, this is student learning centered. This is HARD and difficult for secondary teachers, especially to do (MacMath et al., 2017). I know, I realize this. I spent many years in a secondary social studies classroom exhausted and praying to the patron saint of teachers (who I later found out is St John Baptiste De La Salle, but I would not mind St Jude of lost causes as a close second! Guiley, 2001) and hoping the principal would not do a walkthrough the next day. It was chaos. It was planning hell. It took hours to do right, and I swear that I got it wrong most days. But as my dear friend, and fellow educator, Nancy Hinkley would tell me: It doesn't have to be great, but it needs to do no harm and help kids. She is right, which leads me to my next point for writing this book.

An observation: school as it is currently constructed is not helping our differently-abled learners be successful. The stats are wretched. Most students labeled with a disability will drop out of school. The graduation rate for students with disabilities is a national emergency. Why? Because we do not spend the time to help students see the connections among their 7-8 subjects a day in a secondary school (Wood et al., 2017). We do not allow students to express their thoughts and ideas in creative manners that do not involve pens and paper. Yet most jobs today do not require you to write long discursive essays on Shakespeare.

Before you get mad, **<u>all students must have access to a rich and challenging and creative curriculum</u>**. The system needs to be fixed. So my brother Nick is very smart and talented. While I went for the academic stuff, he went and did the practical stuff. Nick repairs technology daily. I have been known to say "Help the internet is broken!" Nick refurbished a house by himself. He learned to plumb, wire electrical, HVAC, level a floor, and put up drywall. While he was doing this, I learned how to create a historiography of American Education using neoliberal policy lens (Jakubowski, 2019). My mom and dad say they love us both equally, but they call him when something needs to be fixed around the house. Just saying!

Thought Break

Throughout this text you will be given an opportunity to take a break and write your ideas down in a safe place. Now this pains me, because I HATE writing in books. I DO NOT highlight, underline, or star in a book. I have no idea why, but I really never do. Please, do as I say and not as I do. WRITE, <u>underline,</u> circle, star, whatever you need to do, unless this is a library book, then please use sticky notes. My librarian friends will thank you!

*Question: What is one occupation you wanted to be as a child? If you can't remember, and you have children of your own, what is one occupation your child would like to be?

What are some of the STEM concepts that occupation deals with? What are some humanities concepts the occupation must deal with?

How aware am I in my classroom of my students with different learning needs?

What is one accommodation I really should make to help my special needs students?

Conspiracy or Policy?

I need to reiterate: this book emerges as I have seen a death of the humanities and civil discourse. The field has been devastated. Major universities have closed foreign language departments. Historians, social scientists, and humanities scholars are reduced to adjuncting and qualifying for food stamps. Museums are strangled by the lack of donors and visitors and school children. People use GPS (Global Positioning Systems, or map apps on their phones) to travel and don't consult with paper maps. Fake news travels across the internet and destroys reality. The National Council for Social Studies, librarians, and others have had to produce materials to help teachers help students evaluate and suss out fake news. It was bad enough growing up when we were told in school not to cite the *Encyclopedia Britannica* as a source! Now internet search engines are delivering stuff worse than the supermarket tabloids! Many places do not see the value in a social science or a humanities background. Some research studies cite that most Americans don't read a book after graduation from HS or college (Hess, 2019). People died for the right to learn how to read and to gain access to books! I want to show you how we can revive history, geography, economics, sociology, and civics by working with and integrating with art and the STEM fields. We don't have to be enemies. We need to be allies. I wish to draw the American attention to Great Britain and the BBC. There was a wonderful series on the BBC that ran for 20+ years about archaeology called *Time Team* (Bonacchi, et al,. 2014). Each week, a team of archaeologists would work on uncovering some aspect of British history over a three-day dig. The lead members of the team would explain how the area developed, would posit theories, and demonstrate evidence to the audience. The host would "everyman" the conversation to keep the academics in line, but it was history, it was science, and it showed the intersection of a wide range of disciplines as they connected to let people into their nation.

A second great example of the living history that the BBC has done over the years is the *Supersizers Go* which took two people through a week-long undertaking of the food that one ate during the time frame examined. The group looked at the culture, the cooking, and the food and drink of the time period (Bonner & Jacobs, 2017). Very HEARTS in its approach. There are a number of YouTube stars who focus on history, including the vintage Egyptologist, Bernadette Banner, Joseph Townsends & Sons, and others. Most of the YouTubers focusing on history do "living history," and the programs integrate the actual day-to-day efforts along with theory. When looking for examples of theory and practice, the number of amazing people doing profound work is quite extensive, and the main aspect of their efforts are the interdisciplinary nature of the products. The best presenters combine macro level with micro history and living, experiential history. When people are interested in learning, it occurs when they can actually do something, be engaged in something, and create a piece, such as the historical item preservation efforts of "The Workshop " by BBC.

People are very interested in history that is engaging, provocative, tied to their own reality, and reflective of their own experiences. Genealogy is at an all time high, with Ancestry, 23andme, and a multitude of platforms offering services to find family records in official sources, but also offering DNA tests to allow people to meet distant relatives. There are popular TV shows such as "*Who Do You Think You Are?*" and "*History Detectives*" that take a celebrity or an everyday person and help them solve a mystery using not only the humanities, but the hard and social sciences (Kramer, 2011). A recent book, *Ancestor Trouble,* discusses the search for family, genealogy, and the realization that the past is not as pretty as some family stories are transmitted. The book is fascinating, and discusses everyday people coming to grips with their ancestors' role in history (Newton, 2022).

Controversy, but HEARTS-Related

Until recently, J.K. Rowling was a well-accepted author creating fantasy which included the *Harry Potter Universe*. Unfortunately, the author published disturbing and abusive comments hurtful to a wide range of people. I believe that the balance of work by Rowling created a "good" in the world, but the comments and standpoints are "bad" and folks need to be aware of this fact (Whitson, 2021).

In *Harry Potter*, the story of "The Boy Who Lived" brought us to the wizard universe, where we learned about sciences, technology, math and wizardry. While not technically engineering, the wizard world she created got students excited about reading and learning. Her efforts to discuss biology through the magical creatures led to the *Fantastic Beasts and Where to Find Them* part of the series. Rowling also used history as backdrop to her books as she discussed the legend of the founding of each house in Hogwarts. She made history an ever present part of school with the paintings. Rowling made "nerd" cool, as Hermoine Granger researched in the library for the answers to pressing problems. I see, almost 15 years later, the influence Harry Potter has had on engineering students. They love the idea of a school where you can learn the secrets of the universe (Granger, 2020).

Thought Break

*What other fantasy or science fiction works could you incorporate into your HEARTS program?

1. STARTING WITH SOCIAL STUDIES

I now turn to the integration of HEARTS and what I envision for the rest of the book. Each chapter will focus on integrating the major areas of HEARTS. The National Council for Social Studies has also helped humanities teachers in trying to find ways of examining science themes in their students' studies. And as witnessed in recent times in the United States, there is a dearth of teaching about critical thinking, civics education, and evidence analysis, in my opinion. As teachers in K-12 and higher education, we MUST recapture the curriculum integration approach, not rush students into early specializations, and allow for better critical thinking skills.

Our efforts start with the national social studies C3 standards: College, Career and Civic Life. When we look closer at the C3 standards, we find that Dimension 2: Applying disciplinary tools is one of the key areas to focus on this integration. We have four key areas: Geography, Economics, Civics and History (Grant et al., 2015).

Geography

As social studies teachers know, geography is a social science which intersects with the hard earth sciences. Geography is a key science in social studies. It is critical. Rated as a top four of the disciplines in social studies, students need to use it to become informed citizens (De Blij et al., 1997)

Geography is defined as the study of our world and our people. The field relies upon science and humanities to tell its story. A good student of geography will look at the mountains, lakes, rivers, and precipitation in a given area. But they will look deeper, at how the area's economy functions, or the type of governmental structure which exists in the shadow of the hills and valleys. The geographer may swim even deeper and tell how humans have tried to impose their will on the area by farming in terraces or creating a reservoir to water the farms. Mark Monmonier (2018) and H.J. De Blij are two geographers who exemplify a rich tradition of integrating the human and natural sciences together. Geography has moved farther into the use of science to explain some of its efforts in the adoption of Geographic Information Systems or GIS.

In the field of archaeology, the use of geophysics as exemplified on the BBC's long running show *Time Team* is a perfect example of the marriage between the humanities and STEM work. For those of you not familiar with the efforts of the Time *Team*, a group of British archaeologists would converge on an archaeological site for three days to answer a question. Before they began digging, the team would have a group of scientists using ground penetrating radar to see if there were any physical abnormalities present that would help lead the archaeologists to a successful dig site. *Time Team* used the geophys in a combination of HEARTS to heighten the archaeological efforts that were underway.

Geography is helpful when talking about weather and climate. For much of history, there has been an ongoing tension between human civilization being affected by climate and humans affecting climate change as a result of our concerted or byproducts. The climate areas of the Indian Subcontinent most assuredly impact the civilizations from that region. If anything, students exploring World History will discuss how the monsoons affect the world in the Ganges and Indus river valleys. The monsoons drench the plateaus with wet winds from the Indian Ocean and then turn and direct dry winds from the Deccan Plateaus and Himalayans. Hindu society in India needed to adjust to the wind to build its society. The Ganges River overflows its banks during monsoon season and causes massive damage in Bangladesh. A second example of the monsoon winds involved trade from the Indian Subcontinent to Africa. The trading states along the Indian Ocean used the monsoon winds as a way to connect and exchange goods between two continents. The traders between the two regions developed a strong and lucrative spice trade that would enhance the wealth of the African coast and the Indian subcontinent (Grant et al., 2015).

In ancient Egypt, the yearly floods of the Nile were a central aspect to the Pharaonic Empire. As the ice and snow and tropical rains from the deep part of Africa made their way along the Nile, overflowing banks brought good farming soil to the empire. This allowed the Pharaohs to raise an empire, but have enough people moved away from subsistence agriculture to build the tombs in the Pyramids, work math and astronomy, and begin to develop medicine. The development of a civilization in a central crossroads of the world would create an empire engaged in interactions as far away as Europe and Asia (Grant et al., 2015).

Geography and the study of climate change leads me to think about the Vikings. Why did the Vikings sail out of Scandinavia? According to a number of scientists and historians, the Vikings had grown when the climate shifted. Then with a collapse of the warmer weather period, so many farmers and families were affected by the increasingly difficult weather in the Upper European world that they needed to find additional resources. So they sailed. And raided, and took over good chunks of Europe. The Norsemen landed in the Italian peninsula and Northwest France, and invaded Ireland and Scotland. Their efforts to explore led them further west to Iceland, Greenland, and North America. Leading researchers across the European and North America are in agreement that these early explorers were critical in passing information on to other peoples about lands to the west. The Normans impacted Europe even further by giving rise to the political struggles in England which changed the way Christianity monasteries protected ancient knowledge. The raids further impacted the history of Europe by setting up new dynasties in the English monarchical system and leading to the impact of the Russian views about Western Europeans (Somerville & McDonald, 2013).

Our students need to have connections drawn between world climate change in history and the action of peoples to adopt or move. Great migrations across Africa by the Bantu speakers changed the history of Africa. In the Saharan Desert, this once lush, green space, changed, and created a foreboding hostile environment. The desert is getting bigger, and engulfing marginal lands across northern Africa. In and of itself, the changes in African continental climates are further exacerbating already devastating human misery, as famines are again present in regions which once had enough agricultural production to trade. The chapter on geography will go into detail, and we will journey through integrating geography and HEARTS disciplines into a comprehensive curriculum for students at school .

Thought Break

What are some local examples of geography that intrigue you or you wish you could deep dive into in your classroom?

Economics

HEARTS and economics are critical to understand the world. Interweaving our interdisciplinary approach will create better citizens. As we explore the combined areas, these connections will allow you, as a practicing teacher, an opportunity to see specifically how students need to understand the specifics and the cross areas of economics and HEARTS.

As a recent book *The Masters of Craft* (Ocejo, 2017) revealed, the American economy has moved in such a direction that people are tired of mass produced items. Americans are more interested in how crafting, or bespoke production, works. Consumers want to understand how the makers of items enact their expertise as craftspeople. Local focus on crafts and agriculture can create a vibrant economy which highlights quality and precision in a world of mass production. The book tells the story of how quality, small batch, and local based economic work encourages workers, consumers, and producers to recapture the love of effort. When we as teachers look at economics, we need to understand how economics relates to history, geography, civics, and the STEAM fields. It is critical for teachers, especially in the secondary (7-12 and college), to help students understand the complexity of economics and HEARTS.

So what is economics? For a number of professionals, the field has been described as too math heavy and very technical. While this is true, with a heavy reliance on statistics, economics is the study of distributing scarce resources. Economics drives and influences every other field, and many practitioners in other professions realize, often far too late, that they need an understanding of economics in order to succeed in other areas. Often business schools, social science schools, and liberal arts schools fight over where economics belongs. In essence, economics is the study of and attempt to analyze the needs and wants of scarce resources by people, organizations, and societies. Economics has evolved from the paleolithic stone age of bartering up through the development of "value" in items and goods that are abstract, such as gold or gems, through the development of coins, money, and "near money" like paintings, objects d'art, antiquities, and land, labor, capital, and entrepreneurship (Walstad, 2001). Economics is the study of how resources are used, saved, or wasted. To that end, economics as a field can be examined in micro and macro settings, or people and large complex systems. Economics studies motivation and rationalizations, and how people decide to vote, associate with, or leave people. Economics drives every single other field in some way shape or form, and it is one of the least understood areas of study.

Teachers working in economics, especially K-12, find themselves teaching children time, the concept of money, value, and worth. Schooling is, writ large, set up to train students to reduce their immediate desire for gratification by trading opportunity cost. The theory goes, the more education you receive, and the more income you make, the better off your existence later in life (Robeyns, 2006). Education also describes values and examines how the stock market works. The idea and concept of taxes are covered, but usually in an esoteric fashion. Often economics as a pure academic field is divided from the "life skills side" of student existence with home and careers, or business courses teaching students how to, using a popular phrase "adult" after school. Checking accounts, grocery lists, and career exploration are divorced from the micro and macro economics of the social studies academics (Robeyns, 2006).

I believe, as I will show later in the chapter, that this bifurcation has led to a number of misunderstandings and confusions. Students at the age of 18 are often treated as adults, yet understand very little what that entails. As an 18 year old, the simple concept of how work translates into economics and how political parties use economics to make policy decisions seems remote to a newly minted adult, until they take out financial aid loans or need to work to afford school. With the practical and theoretical knowledge so divided, many times people have no idea how to understand and ask legitimate questions about a myriad of subjects. All of which is required to go about buying a house or car, or understanding grocery expenses or cell phone plans.

Thought Break

How do you work in economics in your classroom?

*What do you wish you could know more about in order to strengthen your economics education curriculum?

Civics

The frustration that emerges after feeling the world is taking advantage of you economically often leads to the need of the third major area: Civics. Since the early 2000s, a struggle has emerged in the United States, with many pundits calling for better civics education, while active efforts to defund schooling have resulted in a focus on literacy and math out of context from the historical and civic roots (Littenburg-Tobias, 2021).

Civics and calls for civic education have become immensely more relevant since the 2016 presidential election and the 2020 incited riots at the Capitol. A number of Americans have an unhealthy belief in a false narrative about how elections work (Littenberg-Tobias, 2021). They do not understand voting, citizen participation, and the rights, duties, and expectations for an American in the United States. Partially caused by the overwhelming amount of complex information given to students in K-12, and partially caused by attempts to obfuscate citizen rights, Americans are confused. And the fault line happens along the college degree line. Almost every American attends/graduates K-12. A number of Americans attend some college classes. Only 25% of the population has completed a bachelor's degree. Folks who do not have a bachelor's degree are more likely, statistically, to support the incorrect narrative of how voting works. Most Americans who have a high school diploma or lower are most significantly not interested in voting, becoming involved in other ways in the electoral process, or attending to newspapers, authenticated websites, or other forms of media which portrays events from a non-partisan viewpoint (Littenberg-Tobias, 2021).

There is also a significant issue in the United States where academic work and education have, in many communities, been viewed as a burden on society. In two seminal works, *Anti-intellectualism in American History* (Hofstadter, 1963) and *The Death of Expertise* (Nichols, 2017), authors indicate that "everyday Americans" often refute, debunk, or ignore experts. Candidates are often encouraged to "speak to the people." In federal legislation, education materials must, by law, be sent to parents in "plain language" in order to explain what the schools are supposed to do according to bureaucrats in D.C. Authors have repeatedly found, and Campbell Scribner, Jack Schneider, Amy Azano, Catherine Biddle, Kathy Cramer, Erin McHenry Sorber, and I as examples, that in debates about schooling, a number of residents along a conservative ideology want less education, with a focus on the basics, and demand schools need to do less, cost less, and be more like the education of thirty or more years ago (Cervone, 2017). In Sherman's (2021) work on rural America, people who work with their hands, doing real, manual labor, are viewed as engaging in real, honest work. The same sentiment applied in Cramer (2016) interviews with rural Americans. The interviews in Cramer (2016) work found that rural residents believed that teachers, bureaucrats, and others did not understand or value the work rural Americans undertake. In Carr & Kefalas (2009), teachers believed that their role in rural schools was to educate those who would leave for bigger, better, and more important roles in urban settings. The rural residents were enraged that the schools were devaluing, in their opinion, the rural lifestyle and resource extraction efforts that families had engaged in for generations.

With complexity, artificial Intelligence, data analytics, and bioengineering have entered into America's daily life. Algorithms, social media, and data scraping explode to tell people what they should like, what they should buy, and how people should change their lives. Fitbits, Google, Samsung, Apple, and other companies are buying and selling small data in order to combine these facts into trends and make money. Just as McDonalds is a real estate company (yes it's true!) (Park & Glascock, 2010). Civics and business and STEM collide into a mix, and decision-making points emerge concerning basics of security, privacy, artificial intelligence, and science writ large.

Civics and STEAM go hand in hand, as ethics are part of civics, and regulations to ensure safety, all civic based ideas, must be part of the STEM world. Additionally, civics addresses many whys behind conservation, environmental protection, worker rights, and consumer rights. It is essential for civics education and STEM to merge into HEARTS as educators progress. If educators, residents, citizens, and parents want students to learn how to live well in society, then an overwhelming need for integrated teaching in the area of HEARTS is necessary to ensure that our children grow into educated and engaged members of society.

Thought Break

How can the need for teacher control within the classroom balance with the needed growth of student independence?

How do rules in your school enhance civic engagement?

History

Our final, and most complex area of integrated curriculum is history. History itself is a very complex subject. The two major historical associations, the American History Association and the American Organization of History, both have over 100 classifications of the work historians do. In K-12, the area of history is a little less complex, with history divided into macro-, or world, and micro-, or the self and your immediate family, as the subject of study. The K-12 world divides history into essentially American and not American history. This is problematic, as children often do not understand how events happen simultaneously in different parts of the world. Children often do not grasp the complexity of history, because the ideas are abstract, and developmentally, it is often difficult to help children in this growth. Authors like Jill Gradwell, S.G. Grant, Kathy Swan, Bruce VanSledgewright, and others have tried to propose the pedagogical solution to the problem of teaching history, but as Sam Wineburg, and his students of the Stanford History Education Group have revealed, the skills of an historian, and the teaching of history and process are often conflated with content (Wineburg, 2010). Lesh (2011) wrote a phenomenal book, *Why won't you just tell us the answer?* exploring the problem of history. The subject is hard. Students think that history has a right answer, but there isn't one! The efforts to reveal the "right answer" in history often lead towards crisis, as a "whig" or ever upwards trajectory in history does not really acknowledge the negative, or difficult times, events, and histories of people who are marginalized (Wineburg, 2010). Second, in many US states, legal challenges to "ethnic studies" and non-centrist histories are hurting academic freedom and students' ability to study history beyond the patriotism narrative that many nationalists find appealing (Edweek, 2021). In the opening days of 2023, the assault on multicultural books, history, and society has seen the Florida governor bully the College Board into retracting a number of AP Afro-American history units. Anti Critical Race Theory bills introduced in almost 40 state legislatures have seen teachers, professors, and librarians fear the climate of trying to teach or provide resources to students who are diverse (Langreo, 2023).

History is an evidence-based, narrative, cause-and-effect analysis that moves beyond names and dates. Facts form the basis of history, but the story emerges from interpretation. As Lesh, and others point out, interpretation requires weighing evidence. Judging the truthfulness or completeness of evidence is hard. Narrative requires perspective taking, a skill that only develops as children age. Historians weigh *why* an author created a source. There are motivations for creation. There are reasons behind why an event belongs in a narrative, or is seemingly created for unclear reasons (Lowenthal, 1998).

History, as practiced as a social science, requires a separation from the scholar and the influences. Yet, history educators face a greater challenge: How to construct meaningful, engaging, and relevant lessons for our students. We are challenged by this mighty quarrel among the goals of pure science and the demands by a nation, state, or locality to honor the roots of a community. We know, abstractly, that history happens to many different people, just as we are the product of history. It takes a significant amount of study and critical thinking to understand how self centered humans are, especially about their experiences. What you lived through may be totally different than what I lived through. As educators, we must realize that the skills of historians are hard to teach to people up until they are older (Lowenthal, 1998).

We cannot just teach history better. We need skilled practitioners who know more than just the dominant narrative. We need educators who can place aside their own identities, values, and beliefs and teach history as a way to understand the past. And the past is difficult, and full of warts and triumphs. History cannot exist as an unquestioning narrative;

history needs to organically emerge from examination and reflection through the lens of existence and experience (Wineburg, 2010).

Until the United States teaches history better, our citizens will not understand how we came into being as a patchwork nation.

2. SCIENCE, RIGOROUS THOUGHTS

From our perspective as educators, we need to understand the broad number of science content students encounter in school and curriculum. It's not just science; it's subfields! We see biology, chemistry, physics, and earth sciences. Our four areas have subfields which are complex and require studies well beyond the basics of K-12. Our colleges try to introduce future teachers to the basics of science fields, but many of the courses and requirements are cursory, and are not truly in-depth. As pundits have mentioned, and some international testing data shows, the United States does not always do well in comparisons to other nations on scientific advances (Rutkowski, 2015). We also suffer from a huge issue where a number of people do not believe in, nor listen to the scientific advice of many leaders in the field (Delisle, 2021). While we are, as a nation, still leading in many areas of intellectual property development, the nation has imported significant talent from around the world to make up for the dearth of home grown folks interested in STEM fields. We have a leaky pipeline. It is a national emergency how leaky the pipeline is in STEM, with so many members of our society dropping out from finding their place in the academic, and then later, professional world of STEM (Nichols, 2017).

Millions of targeted dollars are spent each year trying to stop the leak (more like a flood) of the pipeline. The US has tried, through policy, to give teachers a stipend to keep them in the science fields. We have tried to train STEM teachers by offering scholarships. We have tried to directly support professional and scholastic societies and granted scholarships to help keep people in the pipeline. Yet the situation is desperate. President Kennedy, after the Soviets in the 1950s launched *Sputnik* into space, declared in his early presidential term that the US would land a man on the moon by the end of the 1960s decade. This "moon shot" created a demand from the federal government via funding to universities and private contractors to do their best to put a man on the moon (Erduran, 2020). And it worked. The US led the space program and the related research fields for almost a generation. Then in the 1980s, funding was decimated, and politics ruled over the scientists. In the early 1980s, to the horror of millions of teachers, parents, politicians, and students, the *Challenger* was destroyed in a post launch accident. It was a tragedy of immense proportions compounded by a twist of destiny (Erduran, 2020).

On board the *Challenger* was Christine McAllife, a teacher who had trained with NASA to raise publicity and drive more students into the STEM field. She and her brave crewmates were killed because the engineers and scientists begged their politically appointed bosses to hold off the launch when a problem with the launch mechanisms were discovered. The engineers and scientists were overruled by the politicians, who wanted the live television coverage and the "splash" of a successful launch. Disaster investigators, and scientists, revealed that when cold temperatures caused compression in the parts of the rockets, the rubber "o ring" seals were no longer functioning, and highly flammable fuel escaped and ignited against the rocket blast of the launch rockets. This is a basic fact of science: cold causes contraction, highly flammable fuels, needed to create the force necessary to escape the gravity fields on earth, once ignited, combust (Erduran, 2020).

A younger reader may also remember that the *Columbia* also was destroyed due to a fire and explosion caused by damage from lift-off upon its re-entry. Older readers may remember that early space exploration was deadly, with test pilots and astronauts killed as the explosions, the calculations, and the science weren't quite matching the realities of what was happening. A basic, fundamental flaw in science was this simple fact: politicians tend to not listen to scientists because there is no concrete answer. There are shades of gray, and probabilities, not guarantees. People are afraid of uncertainty, and want as much certainty as possible (Erduran, 2020). They do not like to gamble.

As I write this book, we are beyond the one-year mark of the COVID-19 pandemic, a once a century virus attack that froze the American economy and the world, and showed real cracks in the United State's economic, political, and social set up. Within the political, scientific fact, reason, and research we called into question, and basic principles of science were tossed aside by politicians to have their narrative win on the election stage. And the narrative cost 800,000 lives as of December, 2021 (Murphy et al., 2021).

Biology, chemistry, physics, and earth science are all interrelated, and all support each other. These four science disciplines create a way to examine the world in a structured, systematic way. While most scientists would argue that the overarching branches of sciences are unique, and this I agree with, for HEARTS purposes, the four areas will suffice. Each area has nuance, and detail, and has unique subareas, but the four general areas are a sufficient starting point for our purposes. Let's look at the four areas in some detail.

Biology

Biology, the study of life, relies upon every other science for its foundations. Living creatures need inert materials, like nutrients, energy, and environmental elements such as oxygen and carbon dioxide to survive.

The study of biology (Kratz, 2017) is in many ways the study of how living beings conduct chemistry and physics in an environment (earth science). Biology looks at dividing living beings into groups, and then naming individuals uniquely as possible (taxonomy). The scientific method in biology explores how different "kingdoms" of life are different yet contain similar structures and details. The debates in science, still evolving, identify domains (three, with multi-cell organisms being one of the three). In kingdoms, multi-cell animals are different from plants, and fungi are different from the first two. Microorganisms constitute the rest, with biologists specializing even further from the top tiers of the classification system. Macro biologists and microbiologists look at the world differently, as do animal experts and plant experts. Biology, a rich science, creates opportunities to examine life, and how people, a part of that life system, come into being, live their lives, and then pass on. The interaction with science and social science is interesting, especially in fields like archaeology, anthropology, and history, where understanding how life works is especially influenced by psychology and interactions with biological resources for survival (Kratz, 2017).

In our Covid-19 world, people need to understand biology, germ theory, and hygiene that emerges from biology. People question vaccines, and public health related to eating better, like less sugar and fast food. Why have, especially Americans, disregarded basic biological sciences? It has a lot to do with what Tom Nichols (2017) calls in his work the "willful ignorance of expertise." Other examples include Americans not understanding the food production system, especially on farms, and "industrial" farming that has created extreme pressure on the environment, the healthcare industry, and economic well being. Americans also do not understand basic biology of the human body with rest and the need for sleep. Research studies show over and over that Americans, especially high school children, are sleep deprived, and most Americans need a stimulant (coffee) to work because they are sleepy and rest deprived. We need to do a better job of ensuring Americans are taught the critical thinking of biology as it relates to their self care, their diets, and the environment (Kratz, 2017).

Thought Break

Why is science so scary to so many teachers, unless they are a science teacher?

What could be done to better prepare non-science teachers to teach concepts?

Chemistry

The second field I want to discuss is chemistry—a great field, with a ton of pieces so relevant to people! How we color clothes, how we make cars work, the air we breath, and water we drink emerges from Chem (Moore, 2019) and how we address the science behind how the 21st century, including pharma and food, also owes its roots to Chem! Our world is created and ruled by chemical processes, from the tires on our cars to the food flavorings and preservation techniques. Chemistry helps grow more and better crops. People are afraid of chemistry because of the amount of math that a student must learn, but who doesn't love creating a tie dyed t-shirt? Or who wouldn't want to ensure they can remove grease or oil from their dishes or baby ducks after an oil spill (Moore, 2019)?

Our rivers and streams suffer from run-off from pollution from streets, and what is worse, we see algae blooms in many lakes that kill fish and starve other marine wildlife. People need to be clear about how much chemistry plays in their daily lives, and they need to understand, historically, how smelting, electroplating, and fertilizers changed the world. The Green Revolution, a combination of biology and chemistry, increased food yields around the world. This changed the scope of malnutrition deaths in the developing world. As vaccines were created and administered, also a combination of chem and bio, infant death plummeted, and populations surged. Without the industrialization processes of mining and manufacturing, the great economies would have never exploited workers and other nations with cheap carcinogens and pollution in the manufacturing zones (Moore, 2019).

Fuel types expanded, and allowed people to travel faster, as diesel and airline fuel emerged from oil and out performed coal and animal power. The speed at which food products and manufactured goods could move across the world entered a second hemispheric exchange, beyond the initial post 1492 revolution. Now seafood harvested in East Asia appears on dinner plates in London that day. Patients who need an organ transplant can now be the recipient of a donation from across the continent, due to cooling chemicals and high powered fuels (Moore, 2019).

Our pharma practices have resulted in pollution in rivers and water-ways, where the medication excreted from a person results in fish with hormone imbalances, and prozac levels that indicate our waste water treatment plants leak. Humans and wildlife and other creatures are now regularly exposed to benzene from cars and buses, while pollution from the Midwest falls as acid rain in Canada and the lakes of New York and New England (Moore, 2019).

Hydrofracking in the Marcellus Shale region of the Midwest and Northeast has changed communities, the environment, and people. In North and South Dakota, the Tar Sands Oil drilling processes changed by chemistry have resulted in boom towns, where housing is no longer affordable. In Pennsylvania, and the southern tier of New York, community debates over fracking have resulted in calls for succession, as Southern Tier New York Counties, blocked by the state government, demanded the opportunities that Pennsylvania offered of fracking. Elmira, a New York small city once known for Mark Twain, Corning Glass, and early air industry, saw a rapid and massive influx of workers who were sent to drill in Pennsylvania and needed a place to live. In Hornell, New York, a small city west of Corning and east of Olean, fracking has reactivated the original oil and gas industries that helped, along with the railroad, birth the community (Berg, 2010).

In Pennsylvania communities, the groundwater supply has become, in some areas, heavily polluted by natural gas and contaminants. The local services and schools, downsized after years of falling populations, are seeing a surge in enrollment and people who need assistance. The people who work on the fracking rigs and serve as drivers of the large trucks used to service and haul the products haven't established roots.

The roads and transportation systems are overwhelmed and have outlived their usefulness. Large environmental damage areas are a result of the storage tanks needed for the chemicals and the contaminated water supply in the area (Berg, 2010).

In Hoosick Falls, New York, and the upper Hudson Valley, specifically, Fort Edward, New York, the Cold War world politics roosted at home. Manufacturing a number of chemical products in these small, rural, and poor areas of the state resulted in poor environmental practices and massive containment problems. Spills are common, and environmentally devastating. The chemical industry, heavily manufactured in suburban Buffalo and Niagara Falls, New York, as well as upstate New York cities like Rochester, Syracuse, and Utica, have left a legacy of pollution, contamination, sickness, and million dollar clean up bills (Rabinow, 2019).

Students need to understand how the mining industry, especially in the areas of arsenic, and precious metals, as well as radioactive metals, have converted huge swaths of the US in the west into wastelands and no human zones. While our species needs chemicals, and the processes of chemistry, as my father (a retired chemist) says: never lick the spoon, unlike cooking!

Thought Break

*How has chemistry impacted your life, and your students' life? What are some positives chemistry brings into history, economics and politics?

Physics: Laws of Movements

Architecture and construction, as well as decay. The beginning of being, and the transfer of power. (Holzner & Wohns, 2015)

The mathematical expression of existence, physics tells us how solid objects are, how moveable an object is, and what forces represent change on the object. Our greatest thinkers across history were physicists. They examined questions not within a discipline, but across disciplines. Yet physics was, and continues to be, the uniting factor. Newton's three laws form the basis for physics. The states of matter form the foundation for all realities.

When humans seek to understand their universe, a basic understanding of motion, energy, and perception begin with using math to understand why a foot slips on an icy pond, while a mountain goat can climb a near vertical cliff. We seek to understand how heat, trapped beneath layers of fabric, warms air surrounding our bodies, and makes the cool winter much more tolerable. We want to understand how a metal, heated and hit, and then cooled, becomes a sword, while different types of metal when heated will shatter (Holzner & Wohns, 2015).

We want to understand how cars, traveling on tires, through air, are propelled, and also experience drag. We need energy to overcome inertia, especially when an object at rest will stay at rest, unless acted upon by an outside force. For me, coffee helps—but for others, it may physically mean running. Just like when the wind streams against you as you run, or a hurricane lashes the waves onto a beach, energy, motion, and mass all impact our lives. And we, as curious people, want to work together to ensure that we begin to understand and communicate to others the intricacies of our world (Holzner & Wohns, 2015).

We also want to explore other worlds, and ask questions about the world beyond our planet. In order to leave the gravity pull of our world, we needed to understand the chemistry behind the physics, to create a controlled explosion which drove humanity into space. Now, we are faced with an increasingly alarming climate problem, moved from biology and chemistry into physics. Our earth has heated up almost three degrees over the past century, and another degree or two will result in species ending change. Our physics folks are struggling to control our heat blooms and to find ways to target the excess heat to good use, or cool the planet down (Holzner & Wohns, 2015).

Physics can scientifically allow students and teachers to examine not just energy, motion, and resistance, but also architecture. As the Ancient Egyptians, Romans, and Chinese learned, different properties among different building techniques allowed for the creation of beautiful architecture. The bamboo and wooden structures of Asian civilizations survive intact due to the bend, not break abilities in earthquakes. The Ancient Egyptians, using stars, geometry, and physics, created ramps which led to the pyramids. In Rome, the archimedes screw and the construction of aqueducts supplied growing cities with fresh water, and the monumental feats still stand 2000 years later (Holzner & Wohns, 2015).

Physics, in combination with chemistry, allowed for the creation of gunpowder, and that invention, in ancient China, created a powerful tool for celebration and for work. The understanding of physics in Benin allowed the creation of the lost bronze method, and created art forms that have retained their beauty almost 2000 years after creation. The understanding of and combination with other sciences allowed the Egyptians to accurately calculate and create irrigation works in the Nile River valley, creating an empire that inspired awe and became a focal point for other empires. In South America, the Mayans, Aztecs, and Incas used physics to create long bridges and steep farming terraces that allowed civilizations to flourish until acted upon by outsiders (Holzner & Wohns, 2015).

In our own times, physics has found a way into how furniture is molded to allow ergonomic designs for workers who spend their days at computers and sitting in chairs, acted upon by gravity and repetitive motions. We see how standing desks may be better for the spine because of biophysics—or the combination of biology, anatomy, and physics, and seek to understand a "moment" or point when an outside force acts upon an object and creates a break.

Thought Break:

*What are some examples of physics from your daily life?

How would you explain physics?

Earth Sciences

The field of earth sciences includes three areas: geology, astronomy, and meteorology. Let's look specifically at each of these three areas as they relate to building a more holistic HEARTS approach to education. We first look at geology, which is defined as the study of the earth's crust. We then will examine astronomy, which is associated with areas outside the earth's atmosphere. Finally, we will examine meteorology which examines the earth's climate and weather. Of course, earth sciences also includes environmental science, which is a clear mixture of all four of the major science fields presented (Spooner, 2012).

Geology ROCKS! As I have heard a number of times—but geology is more than just rocks. It is also about the formation of mountains, rivers, and continents. Geology is the study of how volcanoes erupt, and streams erode, and islands become covered in the waves of the ocean. The area also explores how rocks are hard or soft, or create the core areas of the economy in a country, or shape the crops in a farmers field. A critical look at rocks can tell a person that an area was uplifted in the previous millennium and gave way under glaciers. Each of us is profoundly influenced by geology, by the attendant earth reshaping from quakes, volcanoes, and erosion. The waves lapping at a beach make for a warm and pleasant afternoon in the summer, but did you know what your sand is composed of? Do you know how coral is formed? Are you aware of the ocean currents? As part of the study of the earth, we see so many unique ways in which there are changes to our realities. In my lifetime, I have seen the geography of western New York shape its past profoundly, what with the Great Lakes and the escarpment and level glaciated farmland. Our geology experts also dabble in biology, as they examine fossils for dating purposes, and have learned a really critical feature about the death and decay of ancient plant and animal life: it creates petrochemicals. The hydrocarbon industry needs geologists to understand how the world exists to find fossil fuels for the present. The geology experts also look at how minerals can be used to create different products from car parts with their engineering colleagues, and the paint on nails and cosmetics on the face of a passenger in the car! These professionals team with all manner of researchers and inventors and creators to understand how radioactive minerals are formed, mined, and used in energy creation, medical devices, and treatment of diseases. A geologist knows a lot about how the locations of a flat open plain are actually the result of serious geological actions by the earth upon itself. They know nitrates, found naturally and extracted in mining operations, occur in specific places and can be re-deployed to increase a food crop. They work with plant scientists, animal scientists, and agribusinesses to pass materials on to chemists who create different formulations and applications (Spooner, 2012).

Thought Break

How do you use geology in your daily lives? How can you intermix the information into your lessons?

Astronomy

One of the best subjects to discuss with students is astronomy! We can use the stars for a variety of purposes, from understanding how they are created and warming the world, to extraplanetary resources, to how to tell time based on events that happened in the stars above us (Spooner, 2012).

Astronomy allows scientists to fuse a wide range of disciplines together to understand how the outer space of earth really actually impacts the inner space. Astronomy's growth and development have recorded some of the greatest controversies from time in memoria, as the ancient world used stars to navigate and to tell the future. The Persians used stars as part of their travel across the great Silk Road, a major historical trade route stretching from China to the Middle East. Yet they also looked for and, along with the Egyptians, used meteorites to make weapons and religious artifacts that were out of this world. Egyptians, the Indus, and Huang He used astronomy to predict the passage of time for the annual winds, called monsoons, or floods of the River Nile. This timing was critical to food production, as well as the ability of people to be ready for a yearly natural disaster (Spooner, 2012).

Astronomy also paved the way for religious challenges in the Renaissance, as humanist scholars were accused, convicted, and punished because they used observations of comets, meteorites, the stars themselves, and math to challenge the geocentric, or *earth-centered*, doctrine, and restore the heliocentric, or *sun-centered*, model of the solar system. Astronomy has also made super advanced navigation techniques with the use of GPS (global position satellites) and facilitate communication between people, with information spreading at the speed of light.. Farmers need GPS for weather, crop plantation, and application of different chemicals to help their produce. Companies use the sciences for shipping routes, weather routes, and communications, as astronomy allows, in combination with engineering, physics, and chemistry, for a person in Beijing to call Bonn and conference someone from Buffalo about the shipments of goods from the United States to Europe to Asia (Pomeranz & Topik, 2012).

Astronomy has inspired and created new waves of communication, using physics to understand how a radio, x-ray, and sound wave travel great distances. Our television programming, our internet, and communication systems rely on the knowledge of astronomy, physics, and experimentation as we learn how humans can move about the planet and how the impact of global warming, suburbanization, and temperature have changed our environment (Spooner, 2012).

Astronomy has also contributed to many science-fiction novels, art, and entertainment as people look to the stars for inspiration and to induce a sense of awe. There are many franchises set in outer space, focused on interstellar travel, creating a future far more technologically driven than today. From *Star Trek* to *Star Wars*, to Terry Pratchett's *DiscWorld* to Douglas Adams' *A Hitchhiker's Guide to the Galaxy*, we want as a species to know what is out there. We intentionally construct buildings, sacred spaces, and objects to align with the sun or stars, or constellations. We name objects after gods and monsters, and tell myths and legends about feats. We listen for return messages from galaxies far away in the hopes or the dread that we are not alone (Spooner, 2012).

Thought Break

* What about astronomy would you like to use in your life or existence?

Meteorology

Meteorology is the study of climate, weather, and the ways in which physics impacts us as human beings. *Is it raining, will it be sunny, how cold is it?*—three basic questions we ask almost daily. Meteorologists study how weather and climate impact people within an area. These scientists describe how glaciers have melted and the impact of the Santa Ana winds on farming. The weather researchers look at the power of off shore winds to drive turbines and the intensity of hurricanes on our coasts (Spooner, 2012).

Meteorologists must understand physics and chemistry, and biology as well as human interaction with the world. Not just content to predict high and low temperature, these scientists examine what happens to crabs in the Bering Sea as ocean temps rise, and how more fresh water spills off of eroding glaciers. They were some of the first scientists who discussed how gasses emitted by pollution were wreaking havoc on our environment. The scientist community studied and understood the power of acid rain, as it destroyed ecologies in the Northeastern US and Canadian areas. Meteorologists examined how wind and ocean erosion from storms caused by intensified hurricanes and tornadoes, along with river flooding, impacted humans along all parts of the US, from the interior to the coast. The scientists predict and confirm lightning strikes may launch wildfires in parched regions. The exploration of how all manner of climate change and human impact have changed and altered the natural world is clear in their research (Spooner, 2012).

The field is profoundly important in the areas of saving human history, as acid rain is not just affecting the natural but historical. Acid rain has decimated ancient monuments, and erosion is imperiling others. The winds from storms, such as tornadoes and hurricanes, are eating land and structures at much higher rates as the storms race across the world. We see erosion driven by wind uncovering important historical sites, while the drought conditions are drying up deep lakes and destroying wildlife habitat, along with cracking and crumbling structures built in the past. Just like the Dust Bowl of the 1920s, and the desertification of the Sarahra, meteorology studies the impact of weather and climate on people and their spaces (Spooner, 2012).

Thought Break

*How can you go deeper on meteorology in your school?

3. THE MIGHTY SUSQUEHANNA—A STEM AND SOCIAL STUDIES LESSON

The states of New York, Pennsylvania, and Maryland are home to one of the most important river valleys in the Eastern area of the United States. All along the Susquehanna River, small and large cities were established to create markets for farm produce and raw materials heading to market. Starting at its source in Cooperstown, New York, and ending at the Chesapeake Bay, the river provides students and teachers a wonderful thematic point to teach STEM and history. The river has served as a transportation route and communications route, while providing the residents along its banks water, food, and energy.

The Social Studies Standards—college, career and civic life (C3) (NCSS, 2013)—give social studies teachers a wonderful opportunity to refresh their curriculum and engage in some in-depth local case studies. The Pennsylvania social studies standards (SAS, 2017) specify a number of standards where the exploration of the Susquehanna River can form the basis of a case study for students. Especially at the 4-6th grade and the US History from 1850 to the Present, a number of opportunities present themselves to teachers who are looking to integrate social studies and STEM content for their students.

Brief Literature Review

Integrating the curriculum is nothing new for teachers, especially at the elementary level (Walkowiak et al., 2017). There are natural connections between science and math, and ELA and social studies. The creativity of the teacher comes into play when integration occurs across "natural" discipline lines. We are beginning to see these movements in the STEM to STEAM literature which is emerging. Harrison and Parks (2017) ask science teachers to integrate their content area with writing. In social studies, we have been integrating our disciplines with writing since the founding of the discipline. Some examples include work by De La Paz et al. (2017) and Nokes (2017), which focus on writing in the history classroom. The C3 Standards require students to write and present their findings in order to engage in the apprenticeship within the disciplines of research and sharing findings.

This chapter presents a brief, in-classroom, real-life example teachers can use to teach the social studies standards for the Northeast using the Susquehanna River and integrate STEM into their lessons.

Classroom Example: Combining Social Studies, Earth Science, and Math

The C3 standards ask students to examine human and environmental interactions (p. 40). Science standards ask students to investigate the geology of a region that impacts the creation of river valleys. Math standards, both Common Core Learning Standards and Pennsylvania state math standards, ask students to plot and compute distances between two points on an x and y axis. By combining the three content areas, students can explore basic data on the Susquehanna River Valley, how it was created, and how it's impacted humans.

Classroom Experience Steps:

- First, have students create a grid on the map of latitude and longitude. - This is your x and y axis.
- Second, have the students measure the length from the northernmost point of the river in Pennsylvania to the southernmost point. Have students identify cities and villages of importance, and have the students use rulers as well as math equations to find distances from the river to the cities, or along the x-y axis.
- Third, have the students research what types of soil/rock formations are along the Susquehanna River Valley, or your local watershed. If possible bring large samples into the classroom of these rock types and have the students conduct an erosion experiment on the rocks. The class can do this by measuring the depth of the groove the water creates in the soil in a sand table, which a science classroom should have. An alternative to this experiment is having students collect runoff and the sediment within the run off and see what the ratio to particulates and the water was. Students can then graph the results from different speeds and volume in an experiment on different types of soil and rock. The teacher may wish to take students on a field trip to see some of the river valley features. If a field trip is not possible, YouTube and other media sharing sites online may have video of the river and its banks.
- Fourth, have students identify and chart the types of materials which are transported along the river. Have the students compare these materials with historical examples of produce and goods sent along the Susquehanna from the past. Jones (2014) uses the energy resources industry to describe the River's past. Shaw (2014) uses canals as the basis for his analysis of trade and transportation in the region.

- Fifth, have students begin the process of investigating the native nations who lived along the river. Have the students design using materials from the area a scale model of the houses or tools the indigenous people used. Have the students calculate the amount of resources needed to support different size villages which corresponded with the historical village location and sizes. Have students calculate caloric values of different types of food products which were grown or harvested. While an older reference, Wallace (1961) may provide a good starting point for teacher and student research on the natives of Pennsylvania. A more current work by Richter (2005) may be an excellent research resource for students as well.

- Sixth, have students do an in-class report and reveal to their classmates what was found. The classroom teacher can ask students to create reports from their group discussions on their investigations into the River. Further, poster sessions across classrooms may allow students an opportunity to present to peers. Technology allows students to create websites or podcasts or YouTube videos about their findings. If the teacher wanted to add a civic or service component, then students could investigate pollution and clean-up efforts. The class may wish to adopt a river section or one of its tributaries and conduct a cleanup project.

By making the Susquehanna River the focal point of an integrated unit, students and their teacher can meet C3 Learning standards in social studies, math and science. As teachers become more familiar with the River basin, and the standards, they can add layers to the unit, and include the artistry of the river, the biology of the river, and the written poems, stories, music and cinema of the river. Social studies and STEM fields can become closely integrated into a HEARTS acronym. It is good, sound educational practice to integrate content areas where applicable.

Thought Break

How can you use your local history, geography, and science to create an interdisciplinary unit?

4. CROSS-DISCIPLINARY INVESTIGATIONS

In education, calls for cross-disciplinary investigations are loudly, frequently, and incessantly sent to teachers, college faculty, and education in general. Rarely, practitioners are given space, compensation, and training on how to accomplish the critical task of "breaking down silos." In my own area, social studies, college level colleagues are reluctant to work outside of their established disciplines, such as history, economics, sociology, or political science. Social studies is, frankly, controversial among college faculties in the disciplines that were combined into K-12 social studies. At the college level, a professor is an historian, or a geographer or economist, or sociologist. I recently learned interdisciplinary researchers have difficulty in publishing, a major career activity required for faculty. Many outlets, such as research journals, tend to publish their specific niche, while other specific interdisciplinary journals are often viewed as lacking the prestige necessary in the ever increasing demand for more and better scholarship placement.

An example of the "business" side of education are the proposals to eliminate general curriculum requirements from college degrees. Governors and legislatures across the United States are proposing eliminating humanities and social science, and possibly fire, arrest, or fine teachers, librarians, and faculty members who engage in these areas (Towrek, 2013). The proposals follow reports from the American Historical Association and others that faculty in humanities and social sciences are essentially half the size of departments 20 years ago (Bruggeman, 2023). If students who are attending K-12 and college are no longer exposed to a wide range of information, then when those people move into teaching, stronger professional development will be required to "fill knowledge gaps."

The Need for STRONG Professional Development

This chapter will examine work I did as leader of integrating HEARTS in a large urban school district. We needed to change the internal professional development model that divided content area teachers (social studies) from the support services teachers (special education and English language learners). I describe the steps which were taken to examine the data from student achievement tests to inform the professional development plan. I then discuss the actual professional development model using the text *The World that Trade Created* (Pomeranz & Topik, 2012) as the central focus for the yearlong professional development program implementation. I found teachers who engaged in content-based professional development gained confidence in world history and economic history content that they then communicated to their students in the form of a project.

Defining the Need

The Waterways School District (pseudonym) is one of the largest districts in the urban Northeastern region of the United States. It is composed of over 50 schools, with well over 25,000 children, of whom over 85% live in poverty. The district has not seen success in the past decade, as measured by exit exams for students in social studies courses at the high school level. The passing rates on the exams, especially for students with disabilities and English language learners, are extremely low. Within the Waterways School District, the Integrated Co-teaching model is one of the services provided to special education students. In this model, a special education certified teacher is paired with a content certified social studies teacher in the secondary classroom (Rice & Zigmond, 2000). The pairs are often together for one period, and the number of preps for both teachers can be as few as one course to as many as three different courses. The teacher who supports students who are learning English (ELL) may face a similar circumstance. Previous professional development offerings were targeted towards content area teachers and generally did not include special education or ELL teachers. This siloing of professional development meant that many teachers providing valuable support to students with disabilities and English language learners were unable to keep pace with their general education peers in terms of learning content and pedagogy specific to social studies instruction (Benedict et al., 2014) .

In many instances, the special education (SWD) teacher and the ELL teacher are not prepared to teach the world history courses that the Northeastern Region state mandates all students take. The training and preparation for these professionals is limited . In the teacher preparation programs, the most social studies based disciplines many of these future teachers receive can be satisfied by one course over a broad range of disciplines. In almost all instances in the district, the special education teacher relies on the content teacher to deliver the information, and the special education teacher scaffolds the materials to ensure students with disabilities can access the information and the skills (Ashton, 2014). Usually, the students with disabilities may see the special education teacher during a resource period, where the pair or small group will work on class work or study skills or review material from class. Most of the resources the special education or ELL teachers have in this situation are the textbooks or notes from class. Frequently the special education or ELL teacher does not have the background information required to explain and draw examples to help the students in need. The added pressure of the high stakes exit exams leads to many students who are classified as SWD or ELL seeking assistance from the support teachers. In many instances the students struggle with the content and skills of remembering significant facts that are associated with such a broad range of content (Reich & Bailly, 2010).

Literature

In recent years, a number of high quality studies on professional development for teachers has made its way into the literature. A wide number of studies are available for review, but this paper, for the sake of space, will focus on a smaller number of the most recent studies. As standards and accountability ramped up in the United States in 2001, with the introduction of No Child Left Behind, professional development became increasingly geared towards meeting accountability practices. Meuwissen (2017) examined the experiences of two teachers and their professional development experiences in a high stakes environment. This research found teachers often needed to negotiate between state and district mandates and best practices from academic literature. The study further found that professional development achievements in a high stakes environment might be fleeting with constant administrative and program support churn.

With No Child Left Behind's requirement that districts in accountability develop a formal Professional Development plan with formal events, Thacker (2017) investigated both formal and informal professional development activities. This study examined one department's activities in a large high school. This research found formal professional development can be meaningful if it is directly connected with classroom practice, helping students, and their own personal needs expressed by the teacher. The study further found many teachers value informal learning due to its freedom of choice and the ability for a teacher to shape their own questions and seek information from sources they trust.

There is power to collaborative professional development, and engaging teachers in different departments adds value to professional knowledge. Reisman (2017) studied the need to assist social studies teachers in content and literacy integration. Examining the implementation of the Literacy Design Collaborative, the study found that "...the LDC underestimated or under-theorized the knowledge required to effectively implement the approach" (p. 32). In other words, teachers need a significant repertoire of pedagogy and content in order to effectively implement practices within their classroom.

Some of the most effective professional development designed to assist teachers in gaining additional skill and content is interactive. In a study from a rural school district, Callahan, et al,. (2016) worked with problem-based historical inquiry (p. 229) models to assist in-service teachers design more historical thinking classroom practices. Their results indicated collaboration is key, but it must be long term. Experts in content and pedagogy need to be teamed up with teachers for a three year period of time (Callahan et al.,2016, p. 240).

It is not only content area teachers who are under pressure to increase their pedagogy and content knowledge. Special Education teachers, who work with special needs students, are under pressure as the standards and accountability movement call for increasing achievement among all students (Petersen, 2016). Increasingly, students with disabilities are tested on the general education curriculum. In such scenarios, special education teachers need to acquire additional knowledge in content areas where they are tasked to teach. "Professional development that moves beyond mere compliance and assessment for the purpose of accountability...and provides additional learning opportunities to understand how to integrate their current knowledge, while expanding their knowledge of academic content is paramount" (Peterson, 2016, p. 31).

Additionally, research conducted with special education teachers finds they do not receive the professional development necessary for professional growth and technical expertise attainment. In Benedict et al. (2014) report on special education, the authors found, "Many [special education] teachers do not have access to extended, intensive professional development that helps them develop the knowledge and skill required to enhance their effectiveness" (p. 148). In the article, the authors recommend that special education teachers seek out as many professional development resources as possible, including content area literature.

Gore and Rosser (2022) specifically identify professional development across grade levels and content areas as crucial and necessary to improve teacher practice and student achievement. Familiarity, or at least working knowledge of what each grade level and subject area is responsible for implementation is critical to whole picture understanding of the breadth and depth of curriculum.

Professional Development Planning

Designing a professional development plan to remediate the poor results on the end-of-year exams in social studies became critically important for the students in any district, especially the case study district. The first step, collecting data, helped to drive a professional development model. This in turn led to the selection of a professional learning community, or network, text, and the activities for each meeting. Finally, teachers were asked to create some new artifacts to add to their classroom repertoire.

Data analysis: Two forms of data analysis were undertaken in order to develop the professional development plan. Student achievement analysis and teacher needs assessments were conducted. First, student achievement data was analyzed for the past nine state mandated end-of-course exam iterations (three years 2011-2013). Student data was examined by school level achievement data, defining characteristics of race and ethnicity, socioeconomic status, English language learner, and special education students. The data were further analyzed to examine students' achievement scores on the multiple-choice question section, the document short-answer question section, and the essay question section. Concentrating specifically on the multiple-choice question section, the tests were error analysis examined by specific question and specific distractor selection by students in subgroups. On the world history exam, the analysis indicated students were having difficulty with questions which related to economic achievement indicators and world history (general) indicators. The basis for the analysis was the study used in Reich's (2011) paper on the multiple-choice question portrayal of the Soviet Union. This meant specifically that the students were having issues with broad based questions that could not be fixed in a specific time or space of a particular period of study. For instance, students were unable to correctly answer a question which dealt with trade across time and location. The New York State Curriculum and Resource Guide provides possible examples for study in the classroom which included the Gold-Salt Trade in Africa, the Silk Road in Asia, and the Hanseatic League in Europe.

Additionally, students were confused about basic economic concepts such as supply and demand, as well as scarcity. The second conclusion from the analysis emerged that the students were having difficulty discussing the impact of specific events on the course of human history. They could not provide specific examples. For instance, students were unable to identify the rise of cotton farming in Egypt was related to the Industrial Revolution's growth in England. Students were unable to place the discovery of oil in the Middle East as a factor in conflict in that region.

Again, economic issues emerged as a major concern on the exam achievement score. The most significant problem with this data analysis clearly indicated that students who were receiving specialized support in the form of special education and ELL services were most at risk of not achieving a passing standard on the exam.

The second area of data analysis involved discussions with teachers in the support areas of the school district. Some members of the staff had indicated that they were professionally struggling with the amount of content knowledge required for the instruction of the World History course at the secondary level. Additionally, many of the support area teachers were moved among content areas as the populations of the district ebbed and flowed, so the ability of a teacher to learn the material in the previous year and carry the same assignment to the next year was in doubt. In the past, the district had successfully undertaken a large-scale Teaching American History grant. During this program, a significant number of teachers, in social studies, were trained in specific areas of American History. Some support area teachers had been invited to attend and did, but many more that were new to supporting social studies had not had the opportunity to attend the professional development activities. The teachers during this program had found professional book circles to be especially effective in meeting their professional development needs and enhancing their classroom repertoire. With this in mind, the need to support special education teachers, and the previous success with professional book circles, a plan was undertaken to select an appropriate text and initiate a series of activities to enhance the support of teachers' professional development needs (Monroe-Baillargeon & Shema, 2010). This professional development strategy is most closely associated with the Professional Learning Community model, or PLC. DuFour (2014) describes professional learning communities as a group of educators who seek to expand their own level of professional knowledge for classroom instructional improvement. In the Waterways District, the use of PLCs was common, and teachers tended to gravitate to learning experiences to improve their craft. By offering a PLC to teachers outside of a given content area, a safe environment was created for teachers to examine their craft and seek additional knowledge while interacting with peers. This safe environment is a critical feature of a PLC (Dufour, 2014).

Selecting the Text

Our central text for this professional learning community or network was *The World That Trade Created*. The text was selected for three primary reasons. First, the text was written by two renowned authors in the world history field. Their background creates a comfort level in that materials presented within the text are based on the cutting edge of scholarly literature that will be useful to support teachers who are working with at-risk students. This is an extremely important consideration, as most secondary social studies teachers, and in this instance support teachers, become detached from the historiographical conversations that occur within the college or university setting after they leave for the secondary classroom. There are few opportunities for professional development that will broaden teachers' content knowledge, as many professional development activities are more pedagogical in nature. Second, the text was selected for its variety of materials covered across its chapters. The book is written in a vignette style, with selections of historical events in world history from areas that are often without significant coverage in most standard/traditional world history books. The book is a compilation of essays that were previously written for a non-academic audience in a general circulation press (Giraldez, 2001). Selecting texts that are written in a manner which conveys content information in a tightly-packaged format is important for many teachers who are within practice. Many practicing teachers do not often have time to devote to academic reading when they are trying to balance multiple responsibilities that emerge during the career cycle of a teacher. Third, the text was selected with the idea that the materials presented within the text would give concrete examples for teachers to create lesson- and unit-based materials for their own classrooms. Professional development literature frequently cites the needs for teachers who experience professional development to be able to use content presented the next day within their classrooms (Agulair, 2014). The case studies presented within the book were relevant to the teachers instructing the World History course, and were impactful, in that they directly addressed a need for classroom content and student interests.

Activities and Meetings

The semester professional development plan was created for the spring semester, or January-May time period. June was excluded from the calendar due to the needs of school operations and preparations for final exams. Teachers were exhausted, as well. One area of concern in professional development planning needs to include teacher engagement cycles, or how exhausted teachers are. Before school, after school, weekend, or any time which falls within the 180 day calendar most states require is rife with issues. First, teachers are asked to perform multiple tasks, and the physical, emotional, and professional exhaustion is well documented (Rhodes, et al., 2022). Second, teachers' priorities are often focused on the immediate, or next day lesson planning, emotional needs of students, and their own needs. Third, many professional development activities or events are one size fits all and do not adequately meet individual teacher's needs (Rhodes et al., 2022).

So, what, specifically, did I do? As I recollect (Ellis et al, 2011) the PLC was organized, as such: The professional development group met once monthly for two hours after school. During the first meeting, the participants were given a copy of the text. The teachers were encouraged to use close reading strategies and active reading as they engaged with the text. During that first meeting, the teachers were asked to develop a "KWL" chart for the professional development course, with specific attempts to tie student needs in their classroom into the KWL chart. The KWL is a strategy that is used to activate prior knowledge by asking participants to identify what they "know" (k), "want to know" (w) and "learned" (l) at the conclusion of the activity. This activity allows the instructor an opportunity to gauge what the participant knows and what significant reasons attracted them to attend this voluntary professional development course (Kohler, 2009).

Following the KWL chart, the participants went through the book and identified essays that they were looking forward to reading, and as a group identified sections of the texts that would be read by the group, and sections that would be read by individuals and shared with the group. This "jigsaw" activity is designed to allow one of the participants to become an "expert" in the group on a small subject and share with the entire group highlights of materials that are important, but time consuming to cover (Resor, 2008). The group then created an outline of meetings for the rest of the semester. The group agreed to norms of open communication, confidentiality, and a sense of inquiry about information presented within the text and brought to the group by individuals. The group's assignment was to come to the next class having read the sections and develop a brief five-minute presentation about the content covered in their individual sessions. This pattern of meetings and activities continued for the rest of the semester. In one instance, the group developed a "web" of interlocking events that were covered in their individual readings which demonstrated how events across the globe influence historical developments across continents. A second activity was to find a reading from a non-scholarly source that could be used within their classroom for students to engage with materials. The teachers were especially excited about the food and drink sections of the texts and seemed to gravitate to those chapters as part of their presentations.

Participants pulled materials from magazines, newspapers, websites, and cookbooks as they examined how chocolate, tea, and coffee became such highly demanded commodities within the world trade network. The participants were interested in finding out the historical price of chocolate and coffee, and felt sharing this with their students would help drive home economic trade realities for the present and the past. Finally, the group discussed the culminating project: the development of a unit plan that utilized materials covered within the texts for use within the classroom.

Teacher-Created Materials

One of the greatest challenges of the teacher created materials was encouraging the support teachers to think outside of their roles as "add-ons" in the classroom. For many of the teachers in supporting roles, being the special education co-teacher or the ESL teacher meant taking materials and adopting them to use for "their students." This paradigm resulted in students given second-hand materials that were not explicitly designed to support their needs and learning styles. By encouraging teachers who were usually in a support role to develop materials from the central text in the professional development suited for students with disabilities and learning the English language, a whole new area of creativity was tapped in these dedicated adults. One project that a number of teachers undertook was a web quest link for their students which revolved around trade networks that the text discussed. The web quest is a series of web-based activities for students to examine primary source documents, secondary source movie clips, and audio recordings which allow students to develop a thesis, gather evidence, and produce a product that can be examined against an achievement rubric (Zukas, 2000). The web quest involved comparing the role of the triangle trade in the Atlantic basin with the Silk Road on the Eurasian continent. The students were expected to see which of the two routes had the most impact on different regions that were touched by the trade routes. The web quest ensured that students saw the human element involved in the capture of slaves in both Africa and by the pirates in the Middle East.

The second most popular activity asked students to create a sales brochure for products that were discussed within the text. The activity involved students researching the origin and purpose for many of the labor savings devices that were discussed within the book. The students then had to present their findings to a "Shark Tank" like panel of judges who would "invest" in their product. This project not only allowed students to research, but included presentation skills within their research project. The research design had to include a cost benefit analysis for the community in which the project was developed. The cotton gin was used as an example of how one invention changed both American and British economic systems worldwide.

With the dominance of publisher supplied curriculum materials, and lately the Teachers Pay Teachers (TPT) website, professional conundrums are emerging in the field (Shelton et al., 2022). While shortcuts are necessary, as no single teacher can do "it all," a question emerges: are professional development materials from publishers at standards/grade levels? Lowell, et al. (2021) found "oversimplification" in publishers' curriculum materials. It is not uncommon for publishers to produce state-specific textbooks, aligned to the state education standards, and often the supplementary materials are not aligned with the complexity of those standards. Brown et al. (2023) suggests that teachers need more than the publisher provided resources and TPT in order to provide students with the best possible educational experience.

Evaluating Our Professional Development

Evaluating the success of our professional development was very limited. In order to receive extra compensation for attending, the teachers had to fill out a survey on the sessions. All of the survey questions revolved around fit of professional development, the skill of the presenter, and the materials given to participants. The majority of participants rated the professional development as 4 points out of 5, or good. While an ego boost, this evaluation system did not indicate if change was made in the classroom. Using low pressure walk-throughs and informal emails for six months after the completion of the sessions, I found that most teachers enjoyed the camaraderie of the sessions. They enjoyed the anecdotes presented in the book, and occasionally used one in class. One pair of teachers who participated found significant success with the travel brochure activity described above, and extensively implemented it in their classroom. Further formal evaluation would have provided more concrete answers than anecdotal information from walk-throughs and emails.

A positive outcome came from the English Language Learner and Special Education teachers anecdotally reporting feeling more confident with curriculum knowledge for the content area of world history. The ELL and Special Education teachers were able to use parts of the textbook to shore up their own knowledge of world history and provide interesting examples for students concerning world trade and economics. One of the major goals of these professional developments was increasing teacher knowledge of content.

Conclusion

The use of a long-term (semester-length) professional development opportunity that focuses on providing specialized services to teachers with content support is one of the beginning steps needed in improving student outcomes on state exams. By beginning the project with two forms of data analysis, the author was able to introduce a much-needed opportunity for teachers working with at-risk learners. The first data analysis undertaking, focusing on student performance on testing, gave a clear rise to the need for increased focus on economics and world history for teachers working with those student populations. The second data analysis grouping revealed an understanding that many special education and ELL teachers were unprepared with content knowledge, leading to an introduction of the professional development activity. Then, by creating a professional development climate of mutual respect and intellectual inquiry using the book *The World That Trade Created*, teachers were able to explore a wide range of economic and world history topics and become familiar with content that would then become the basis for a project/unit plan for their students in a state-mandated course with a high-stakes exam at its conclusion. Educational professional development should examine more cross-department professional development events, especially in light that students with disabilities and English language learners are a growing population segment in American schools. Schools need to consider strategic professional development plans when assigning special education and ELL teachers to content-based classrooms.

Thought Break:

*How do you plan on partnering with your team?

5. GAMIFYING HEARTS

Teaching social studies in the common core era poses a wide variety of challenges for classroom teachers. Students demand technologically-based, interactive activities in order to facilitate their learning. Teachers do not always have sufficient classroom time to cover all of the required content and still allow for engaging and in-depth discussions. This chapter examines the use of *Forge of Empires*, an online multiplayer game, as a vehicle for teaching students HEARTS content that is aligned to the National Council for the Social Studies' College, Career and Civic Life Framework (C3) and STEM fields. First, the C3 frameworks will be briefly introduced to the reader, along with core STEM content. Second, the *Forge of Empires* game will be discussed as a way to assist teachers in presenting social studies concepts. Third, some concerns with the game will be presented for teachers to consider in developing C3-aligned instruction. Finally, teachers will be provided with some examples of classroom integration for this game in the classroom.

The C3 Frameworks

The National Council for Social Studies has sponsored the release of the C3 standards—College, Career, and Civic Life (Grant, 2013)—and have encouraged states to adopt the C3 standards for their state. The C3 standards are designed to change classroom instruction into a more inquiry-based model. Within the inquiry model, the teacher and the students find and design compelling questions to investigate historical content in a deep way. The C3 standards also ask students to use disciplinary tools in their investigation of historical inquiries. The areas of discipline include history, geography, economics, and civics. The C3 framework then asks students to evaluate sources and use evidence during inquiry. The final C3 skill is *communicating conclusions and taking informed action*. These four areas of focus in the C3 frameworks provide a way for teachers to ask students big picture questions of social studies in a way which encourages in-depth investigation and reporting out to a variety of individuals (NCSS, 2013).

The economics standards are often the most challenging content for students to master. Searching for a way to assist students in learning about economics from a practical perspective, I came across the *Forge of Empires* website. This game is designed to have participants play in an alternative world that charts the development of humanity through a series of stages that progress by "building an empire."

While the game is more recreational than instructional, there are multiple features of *Forge of Empire* that could assist teachers in helping students meet the C3 standards in their classroom. The game is an asynchronous experience that leads students through historical eras. There are some features of the game that allow students to put into practice some of the concepts which are learned in social studies.

STEM Fields

There are three primary STEM fields *Forge of Empires* covers: science, technology, and applications of research. From the perspective of a teacher attempting to teach HEARTS, the technology tree function shows how technology discoveries "stand on the shoulders of giants" by describing the need to invest in research, and how this investment can be fast or slow, depending on priorities. The technology aspect is revealed in game play, where players learn how technologies unlock abilities and additional game play. Finally, the decision-making, or research application asks players to engage in discovery, and if not careful, they waste resources or opportunities.

Literature Review

Research studies suggest the use of computer games in the classroom can aid in and improve student learning (Kelly & Nardi, 2014; Maguth, et al., 2016; Molyneux et al., 2015; Mullgardt, 2014; Squire & Jenkins, 2004). Boyle (2016) examined literature on gaming between 2009-2014 and found that in the 143 papers reviewed for their high-quality research, the gaming reviews were "used most frequently to support knowledge acquisition," which [seemed] to be a rather pedestrian use of games" (p. 187). Within that study, most of the literature reviewed found that "simulations (14), simulation games (10) and role-playing games (12) the most popular, followed by drill and practice games" (p. 181). Boyle (2016) research clearly shows there is research in the area of game-based learning.

In another research report, Hamari et al. (2016) noted that games which engage the player held a positive effect on the learner (p. 170). Further, the report indicated that the game needed to increase the challenge for the participant in order to maintain the engagement and learning experience (p. 176). As a player progresses in the game and improves their skills and abilities, the game should continue to challenge the learner. This will enhance the learner's experience and improve engagement. This is relevant when considering that many learners feel underwhelmed by the challenge offered in traditional classrooms.

Barab et al. (2012) researched students engaged in a game-based classroom and found that students who become enmeshed in the story of the game were more likely to "[draw] upon their own experience in-game where they were able to be someone who used persuasive writing as a powerful tool" (p.526). Further, their study found students engaged in game-based learning were less likely to be off task when in the classroom setting. This is a bonus when compared to research about student engagement in a traditional classroom that finds students unengaged in the learning experience.

James Paul Gee, most commonly known for Discourse Analysis, has offered significant research to the field of game- based learning. In the work on digital learning, Gee (2014) provides insights relevant to improving student learning in the digital age. By using digital learning tools, and asking students to engage in digital learning, teachers are meeting students in a medium that they are most comfortable, and more importantly, engaged in. Additionally, Gee (2014) indicates that digital learning can help overcome some of the inequality in the educational system by making learning less dependent on place-based experiences and more open to learners.

As technology evolves, students have become adept at using computer-based learning strategies for recreation as well as academic pursuits. The game provides students with opportunities to develop decision-making skills and evaluate the value of a goods or service.

Decision-Making

Forge of Empires asks players to engage in a decision-making process. These decisions revolve around scarcity. Scarcity is communicated to the players on multiple levels. First, the game provides players with a limited area to build their city. The player must make efficient use of the limited area by selecting military buildings, residential buildings, and production buildings. The buildings need to be connected to a town hall by roads, so players must think about transportation in their space allotment. The player must keep their citizens happy by providing decorations, so the city must include civic buildings or decorations, or the citizens reduce their efficiency. The classroom teacher can facilitate a discussion of scarcity in the river valley civilizations by discussing the ways which early river valleys made use of their natural resources, but needed technology to advance their productivity. One example of the concept is the Nile River Valley and the irrigation systems used by inhabitants to increase farm yield. This feature of gameplay aligns with the C3 framework concept of Economic Decision-making (NCSS, 2013, p. 35). Economic Decision-making is one of the foundational concepts in the C3 frameworks. It is a critical skill for students to understand how economic decisions are made at the micro (personal) and macro (community/state/market) levels. Economic literacy research encourages students to research and understand economic decision-making by societies as a way to prepare themselves for the world beyond high school.

The second way scarcity is communicated to players is through the provision of Forge points. Forge points allow players to complete a multitude of actions using the points awarded at a speed of one per hour. Forge points allow players to research additional technologies to advance in ages. The technological advances enable players' access to higher levels of technologies and abilities as the game goes on. In addition, the Forge points allow players to trade for goods, which are representative of natural resources that are then manufactured into products. If the player wants a good that someone else has, they often need to trade using a forge point. Third, the forge points allow a player to build "Great Buildings" that grant bonuses to a player's city. The forge points are needed, along with goods to build the structure. Players often need help in building these great buildings, so rely on donations of forge points from other players to help. These Forge points represent research and development from a civilization. It takes a whole civilization to examine needs and invent solutions to problems. This part of *Forge of Empires* also aligns with the C3 frameworks section on economic decision-making (p. 35).

The third way scarcity is communicated to players is through the production of goods. Players control two of a possible five types of goods on their own. However, in order to advance in the game, players need to have access to all five types of goods. They can manufacture all five types, but at a reduced rate if they do not control the natural resources. So players are exposed to competitive advantage and scarcity of natural resources through the manufacturing of goods. At higher levels, players need lower level natural resources to produce higher advanced goods within their cities. They must decide if they should trade for goods or make their own. This is a decision that requires a tradeoff of land size and the value of making a good produced by the city, as well as having the requisite number of people, coins, and supplies available to make the goods within the city. This part of gameplay aligns with the C3 frameworks and its concept of the global economy (NCSS, 2013, p. 39). This alignment helps students actualize a theoretical concept that many find difficult to grasp. This is especially relevant when social studies teachers examine imperialism with their classes. Studying the success of the Dutch colonial empire or the British Empire in trading allows students to understand how an under-resourced region could gain power over resource rich areas. This concept also holds in examining the Japanese success in economic recovery after World War II. Japan does not enjoy many natural resources, yet the nation has a strong international economy due to its focus on high technology and manufacturing efforts. International trade and comparative advantage are two concepts that this feature of *Forge of Empire* helps students grasp.

Value

Another major concept the game has as its core is value. As the player progresses, decisions are made about the worth of a quest, or a series of challenges that are undertaken for rewards or the worth or value of a building that needs construction. Players need to decide if they value 'Great Buildings' or single buildings from each era. When the decisions are made, the player can gather resources, coins, medals, or a variety of different forms of production for their city as they grow an empire. Players need to balance the value of the coins, productions, and military to ensure that their city is protected from economic problems or military raiding. The player also needs to decide if they will join a guild or a network of players who can support the goals of the player as they grow. This decision-making to join a guild can help bring added value to a player as they progress through the game and provide a support network by allowing players to collaborate with each other through daily interactions. This part of gameplay aligns with the idea of National Economy in the C3 frameworks (NCSS, 2013, p. 36). Decisions made at the national level often impact local economic realities. For example, in the United States, the decision to support suburbanization resulted in the declining urban areas and suburban sprawl. The government used tax codes and subsidies to home builders and owners, as well as states constructing the Interstate highway system.

Players in the game must decide if they will be friendly towards their neighbors in a value decision-making process. Players can ignore their neighbors, can attack their neighbors, or aid their neighbors. Each of the three actions has positives and negatives. When ignoring neighboring players in the game, they do not receive the boost to their city's production that comes from daily help in the form of aiding. Aiding can arrive in two forms: motivating or polishing. A motivation increases the output of coins or production, while polishing helps to improve the happiness of the citizens. If a player attacks the neighbors, then they can win medals in a competition and disrupt their neighbor's production by stealing the value. The player who does the attacking realizes they run the risk of a retaliation and loss of their own production. This game play feature allows teachers to open discussions of imperial strategies that the Romans used in Classical periods, the European and Japanese royalty used in feudalism, and the European Imperial system imposed on the conquest of the western hemisphere to the spheres of influence in Africa and Asia. This part of gameplay aligns most closely with the geographic concept of global interaction (NCSS, 2013, p. 44).

Forge of Empire has an additional advantage by allowing players to experience some level of technological progression through various ages. From an historical standpoint, the technology tree starts at the stone age, and transitions through the bronze, iron, early, high and late middle ages. The player then becomes involved in the colonial age, industrial, and progressive age. The third set of ages, the modern, post-modern and contemporary ages, are next. The three current ages are followed by the tomorrow and future ages. Each time period in technology balances living spaces, or residences, production buildings, civic buildings, decorations, military buildings, goods buildings, and roads. The players need to research the technologies in order to gain access to the technology and allow for increased city size, production, and values in the forms of "Great Buildings" which offer bonuses. This section of gameplay is most closely aligned to economic decision-making (NCSS, p. 35).

The "Great Buildings" are different at each age and give players bonuses which can help the city. The features represent world civilization power and cultural achievements. Some examples of the in-game feature include the Statue of Zeus, the Cathedral of Aachen, the Hagia Sophia, and St. Basil's Cathedral. Acquiring a Great Building requires players to find nine parts of blueprints and have the necessary goods resources available to use. The Great Building then requires the in game tokens to build, usually seventy for the first level. Great Buildings can be improved by an investment of in game resources. Players actively seek to gain Great Buildings as a way to increase their score total, which helps their guilds, and their own rankings in the game. This is again most closely aligned to economic decision-making, but by studying the Great Buildings in depth, the program can be used to stimulate discussion in the areas of history and culture.

Forge of Empire combines competition and collaboration in order to motivate players to engage within the story and undertake the quests of the game. While the game is a business undertaking, it does provide players with some enjoyment while learning about world historical events. The multiplayer function of the game will enable students to engage in "chat functions" as well as general messages. This communication system, in addition to the ability to "friend" and join a guild, can allow teachers to have their students compete against each other, against different classes, and against classes from around the world. Teachers should ask students to reflect on their game play and keep journals of entries which describe the decision-making process which they undertook. The class can then debate decision-making as part of their class wide experience with the game. The C3 frameworks ask students to engage in communication and presentations in written form (NCSS, 2013, pp. 59-62). Extension opportunities will be discussed in the classroom application section below.

While the game does not contain 100% historical accuracy, the wide variety of features does allow teachers the opportunity to engage their students in a competitive, free, and online game. This is especially relevant in a time when many students are using technology for recreation as well as learning. The use of mobile devices and social media have created a whole new learning environment for students (Kimmerle et al., 2015).

Concerns

There are two major concerns with the game: pay for play and the open nature of the communications structure. While the game is free, there are some temptations to pay for access to unique and hard to achieve structures. The game communicates the extremely high value of these items through the resource type of "Diamonds." "Diamonds" can be earned rarely, but usually they are acquired through purchase. The "Diamonds" are used to speed up the expansion of a city, the acquisition of special production buildings, and acquire Great Building blueprints. The second concern with the game is the open communication system that allows players to interact with people in an anonymous fashion from around the world. While the game moderator exists to ensure that a level of civility is kept by players, there is no way to ensure players are kept completely safe and are interacting with only classmates, not communicating across the platform outside of the school. . It will be important for the teacher to ensure that students use the game in a safe manner and not access the pay-for play functions which exist in the game.

Classroom Application

The following questions can be used by teachers in starting their students discussing the *Forge of Empire* game in a World History classroom:

Essential Questions: How does a civilization define resources or value NCSS, 2013, (D2.Eco.1.9-12)?

- Supporting question: When scarce resources are available, what decisions does a civilization make about income and expenditures?
- Supporting question: When your city was small, how did you decide to allocate your resources? What types of buildings did you install in your city?
- Supporting question: How did your exploration of the continent support or hinder your city's expansion?

Question 1: When first asked by the in-game tutorial guides to build a house, what did you think? Did you choose to follow the "quest?" What examples in history can you find that demonstrate how people used different types of shelter to adapt to their environments? (NCSS)

Question 2: When spending Forge points, what was your greatest priority and why? Did your priority shift?

Question 3: Did you aid your neighbors, friends, and guild mates? Why or why not (NCSS, 2013, D2.Geo.11.9-12)?

Question 4: Some of the early quests ask you to unlock parts of a map through spending resources. If you did not make the resources, what tasks did you complete in order to gain resources? Were those resources expensive (NCSS D2.Eco.14.9-12)?

Question 5: When did you need to expand your city? How did you go about expanding your city? What are some examples from world history of Imperial Expansion and what rationale did those states use to justify their expansions?

- Activity 1: Prioritization of space.

In economics, and in geography, we learn that human civilizations have unlimited wants and needs and limited resources. In *Forge of Empire*, you have limited space. Using a section of your city, build a house and a production building. Which one produces more resources for your community? Which type of building is more useful and why?

In your city, build enough decorations to add happiness points to your city. Now build the equivalent amount of streets. Which one takes up more space? Which one of your options costs more? How would you meet the needs of your community in real life if you needed to trade space for productions?

- Activity 2: Select one of the Great Buildings that are available in *Forge of Empire*. Using information provided by the game, create a mini presentation that will convince your classmates that this is the most useful Great Building to build in their city. Then, using five outside sources, discuss the significance, relevance, and importance of this Great Building to world civilization. Your presentation should combine technology and the written and spoken word.

- Activity 3: Researching resources: Each of the eras have five potential resources available to each city. Throughout history, different parts of the world controlled different resources that other regions needed. Select a resource from the game. Research that resource and create the following information that describes why that resource was needed in each society. You may choose from the following:

Name of Resource	Civilization	Trade routes	Impact	Source
Oil				
Gold				
Spices				
Silk				
Whale Oil				
Salt				
Rubber				

Conclusion

In the high stakes setting of today's HEARTS, the opportunity for students, especially those with disabilities or second language acquisition, to engage in activities that are game simulations will help teachers in social studies become more relevant to digital students. *Forge of Empires* provides one such opportunity for students to engage in world history content in a low stakes, high engagement setting. The possibilities for reflecting on individual decisions within game play will enable teachers to discuss economic and historical standards from the new C3 frameworks within their classroom. Students enjoy computer-based applications in their learning repertoire.

While the game is recreational, teachers can use game play to examine some economic and historical concepts in a simulated environment. By examining scarcity, value, trade-offs, and supply and demand, the game can allow students to see in real time how decisions they make can impact the growth of their city. The communication function allows the students to interact with each other in a non-structured way. This feature can facilitate out-of-class learning in a subject that some students find difficult. The social aspect of the game allows students who are not often willing to engage in classroom discussion an opportunity to chat virtually with peers. The application can also be useful for students who, due to medical conditions, cannot attend class with their peers

Thought Break

How will you GAMIFY or use games in your classroom?

6. CEMETERY RESEARCH: HEARTS WITH LIFE!
A CHAPTER CO-WRITTEN WITH NANCY HINKLEY, CAS. MS.ED.

A conundrum of course, how can a place of eternal rest be a place with life? As Nancy Hinkey, my mentor, co-teacher, and co-collaborator and I discovered, students "dig" cemetery research, and often find themselves exploring humanity, history, and science within a community, and the site itself. Let us be realistic, many people find cemeteries grim places, but that is an adult reaction. Students love it! You of course want to be wary of students who may have just suffered a trauma, and offer an alternative arrangement, but in reality, cemetery research brings all the HEARTS fields together in one setting.

History and Civics

A great place to start is with the rules of a cemetery. Understanding what good civic behavior looks like is critical in cemetery research. A thematic unit of burials across the ages is a great place to start and having students look at cultures from Ancient Egypt to the present is a great way to discuss how civilizations care for people. You can tie in major catastrophes like war, the plague, or sanitation, the influenza pandemic, or starvation as ways to discuss demographics in local communities, and how this relates to national and international events (Waring, 2011).

Second, many cemeteries need TLC. As budgets in communities run out, and as small organizations collapse as resources erode, governments are left needing to take over these small cemeteries. In rural areas, many times family plots are on the sides of roads, without much acknowledgement or care. A good civic project is to clean up the cemetery, with assistance from the local experts (Miller & Rivera, 2006).

Identifying and highlighting the accomplishments in life of the resting is a great third project. In many areas, small communities have local celebrities who created a major area or were important, or participated in a major event. The deeds and acts need promotion among the local Chambers of Commerce, as heritage tourism is especially relevant, and people want to see who from their ancestral hometown was a famous participant in history. Honoring the stories of war vets is often left to a number of organizations who have seen memberships fall as demographics take hold. Veterans of Foreign Wars, the American Legion, and others often cannot maintain the graves of the dead or memorialize their deeds without help. The class could place an ignored person, or event, on the map for a local community, receive good press coverage, and feel like they were in the process of doing history (Waring, 2011).

Geography

A critical area of cemetery research is location, location, location. Examining maps, and the features of farmland, waterways, settlement patterns, and transportation routes in the area is all critical to understanding how a community grew and what the "out of bounds spaces" were when the cemetery was created. Many cemeteries were laid out next to churches, often in the center of a community, but as the "Parkland" movement flourished, cemeteries were then plotted outside of a town, city, or village, creating open spaces. Instead of small graveyards next to churches, a large urban oasis of the dead mingled in a park-like setting, with benches, trees, pathways and water features. In Buffalo, New York, the Forest Lawn Cemetery is a perfect example of this movement, set off from the city itself on the edge. Whereas in Sidney, New York, the pioneer village cemetery is right in the middle of the village, taking pride of place next to the library and two major street intersections (Miller & Rivera, 2006).

Geography can also demonstrate how inclusive or exclusive communities were in the past. In major cities, as well as villages, different religions refused to mix even in death. Even deeper, ethnic differences often resulted in different cemeteries of the same denomination, but different ethnicities. Cemeteries can often tell us of the deep, bitter, and destructive hatred towards underrepresented populations, as oppressed religious groups and ethnic groups were excluded from cemeteries and needed to find spaces for the dead (Miller & Rivera, 2006). And not just the distant past reveals this prejudice, as within the 2000s, an Islamic observant community in the rural Northeast was refused permission to start a burial ground in a village due to hatred (Siemaszko, 2010).

The absence of memorials or a formal marker can also tell us of the geography of wealth. In many areas, potter's fields are the final resting place of people who were loved by those who knew them, but were subjected to poverty, disease, or prejudice. A classic example is the Potter's field in New York City, where the earliest victims of the AIDS epidemic of the 1980s rest in row upon row of anonymous unmarked plots. Potter's fields are often found in some of the least desirable land, away from people, and viewed as waste land. This geographical understanding also leads to some scientific questions in our next section (Miller & Rivera, 2006).

Earth, Biology, and Chemical Sciences

As the research journey in cemeteries is part of a HEARTS curriculum, it's really important to discuss some of the sciences. For this activity, I have chosen earth, biology, and chemistry as the three areas to explore in a HEARTS way.

Earth science is so varied, and includes so many topics, including erosion, composition of rocks, weather patterns, and impact of pollution on the environment. Environmental science is often part of the "earth sciences." So let's take a look at some of the areas to stress in your HEARTS adventure.

Pollution patterns in cemeteries are very obvious. We notice that garbage is often wind-swept and blown into brush lines along the edges. Asking students to see what types of physical garbage are present can help them understand how the surrounding environment is impacted by humans and litter. I find that graphing exercises of the type, volume, and extent of pollution is a great exercise in citizen scientists, and the under-resourced locations really appreciate the helping hands.

Many cemeteries also have a very park-like setting, so quite often especially near the edges, where streams, or ponds exist, erosion is prevalent. Your class can see erosion, especially if your class makes repeat trips to the location and measures the "fall." The second way erosion is evident is in the stones themselves. Your students can see weathering on the various markers, and the discoloration from acid rain, and the wear and tear from weathering patterns. A good cemetery board may ask your class to help with a project by actually identifying issues with stones from different seasons.

Third, your students can see how the ground shifts in especially older plots, with the heaving from frost action, or the swelling from rain runoff in different zones. By asking students to explore how "out of plumb level" stones are from the perpendicular, or even the surrounding stones, you have a great engineering lesson!

From an engaging perspective, environmental based earth science can also move into how the stones were actually created. Using the MOHS scale, to identify "toughness," you could discuss with a landscaping/marker company the "waste" rocks so that your class can experiment for different levels of toughness. For instance, we know that nothing beats a diamond for toughness, but the carbon of charcoal fails at the scraping of a fingernail. Students could see what it took for the ancients, the middle ages, and recent present to carve stones, and what type of tools were needed. You could have the students experiment with Mohs scales and waste materials from companies in conjunction with art classes and technology classes to understand how the introduction of machine power made life so much more productive, especially as human muscle is easily tired.

Biology: Our eternal places of rest include a number of birds, insects, small and large mammals, and even reptiles and amphibians. The park-like settings often allow an observer to gaze upon deer, or badgers, or robins, or bees. You can have your students do animal observations and see what happens when areas are in different stages of animal habitat. I, for one, always found it interesting how adaptable animals are and see what plants they like to eat. A second way to help your students see the connection is with plant life. The cemeteries provide in stark detail clear examples of natural versus landscaped environments. Different plants, including ground cover, brushes, trees, and blooming plants all have very different roles and niches. To see the plants and to see how ground cover moves from road beds to tall trees that prefer different types of locations are really critical and very informative for students.

Your students can also measure the type and numbers of birds through visual and song. You can help them see the actual animal, or their prints, or feathers, or nests. The birds create part of the environment, and their place within this cemetery can, along with the plants, and other animals, help students see this location as a place of life.

Chemistry: A hard subject to conceptualize for many students, the ability to work through pH and the impact of chemicals is crucial. In many cemeteries, we see the effects of not only pollution, but natural chemistry in action. Identifying different pH of water supply, looking at pH in soil, and understanding how plant matter impacts different parts of the environment are all lessons that can help students understand the growth cycle. You can help students get a clear image of what different past technologies did to the soil by examining the reaction of leeching near old stones or metallic objects. You can have students understand oxidation processes, which is part of chemistry from examining the metal throughout the spaces.

In sum, a cemetery is a great place to teach some HEARTS lessons in different fields, but how do you prepare students? The next section goes into the details of how to prepare students for what they should be looking at while in the cemetery.

Demographic Data

As students are often unsure how to conceptualize historical events, demographic data can help students grasp the makeup of a cemetery:

1. How old was the oldest person?
2. Who was the youngest?
3. Males versus females?
4. Families or individuals?
5. Life span by decades?
6. Any hint to what happened to the person?

By tying in the events that the person lived through by looking at birth and death dates, your students can begin to see how people lived through different events. And if the local genealogy bug has bitten you or your students, it's always a good idea to look for family connections. Demographic data can also help your class understand based upon the size of stones how wealthy a person was. Do they have a name that is connected locally to a famous street or section of town? Is the plot set off and protected in a special section? By examining some basic demographic data and having students look to see if there are correlations to events from the past, you can help students begin to understand the impact of disease had on communities. You can also ask students to discuss health based on life span, as the agrarian past moved into the industrial revolution.

Thought Break

What interests you about potentially using a cemetery for class?

What hesitancy are you experiencing?

7. THE SHAKING EARTH: RING OF FIRE AND HEARTS

World history and the sciences merge rather amazingly well around the Pacific rim where the cultural influences of the Ring of Fire or geologically active locations on earth collide, literally. As the Pacific plate contacts the other plates in the process of plate tectonics, a whole series of earth shattering reactions subject the peoples living in those areas to a reminder that their culture is influenced by the geology of where they live. I have created some examples below of the impact between the science of the Ring of Fire and the impact on the history and culture of the communities most commonly studied. The inspiration emerges from one book I read in school (De Blij, 1997).

Japan

The archipelago of Japan has, as a case study, a way to show how plate tectonics creates a culture. As an island chain, the majority of Japanese islands are volcanic, and the remnants of plates crashing together have profoundly impacted the environment of the nation. Sacred parts of Japanese culture revolve around Mt. Fuji and the seismic activities of the hot springs and earthquakes. Rice cultivation, religious ceremonies, and building materials use the available richness of volcanic soil, the power of fire, and the flexibility of bamboo as a way to ensure that the impact of seismic activities do not devastate the nation (De Blij, 1997).

Japan's main land is severely restricted on farmland and living spaces, due to the ridge of elevated mountains down its center. Therefore the people have adopted by developing a heavy interaction with the sea and fishing as a major part of their agricultural processes. Additionally, the cities in Japan are heavily built up, and as a result, large skyscrapers exist with land at a premium (De Blij, 1997).

The lack of natural resources on the islands have created an outward-facing people, who have sought through a wide range of peaceful and aggressive tactics the natural resources of others. At different times of its existence, Japan has colonized mainland Asia and pushed for advances in technology as a way to overcome its natural resource limitations. The value of technology and education have led to the nation having one of the highest educational levels in the world. Following World War II, and the devastation of the mainland, the people of Japan went East, into North and South America, to study, to settle, and become part of a wide diaspora. Japan has a history of exchange, except for a period of time when its internal politics created an isolationist nation. One of the leading trade nations in the world, Japan has created an advanced manufacturing and STEM economy which faces an interesting challenge: a decline in population (Shin, 2021).

Following World War II, and with the rising costs of education and necessities, many families in Japan adopted the practice of small families. Most couples only have one child. The economy also faces a severe age issue, as the average workforce age advanced with many fewer replacements. Why did this happen? As the expenses of Japanese living increased astronomically and workers spent a significant amount of time on technology, "hacking" or short cuts emerged which promoted a single person or no child lifestyle. Tourism, an example of middle class status, allowed the Japanese people to explore the world, unencumbered. Competition for schooling, based on tests, increased as families moved resources into tutoring and education. Families sacrificed additional members in order to ensure that positive educational outcomes and a stable career were realities (Shin, 2021).

The culture in Japan is also heavily invested in new technology, and have made significant changes to ensure that safety is a priority. With earthquakes, tsunamis, and volcanos, as well as technology needed to bridge between islands and create usable land from the sea, Japan has emphasized engineering and math and STEM professions. The Japanese have promoted educational pathways across the nation, including utilizing overseas experiences, specifically following the westernization drive when Commodore Perry's visit shook the Japanese leadership out of their belief that the nation was technologically advanced compared to the western nations (Shin, 2021).

Broadening the exploration of technology within the *Ring of Fire*, most of the world's largest geothermal producers exist along the tectonic plates of the Pacific Ocean. Japan, Indonesia, Philippines, Costa Rica, Mexico, and the United States are among the leaders for geothermal energy. Technology also travels into the agricultural realm, as many of the nations along the *Ring of Fire* have a wide range of agricultural production and provide trade resources across the world. In Japan, specifically, the fishing economy heavily relies on the ocean's currents, and rice cultivation needs nutrient rich soil with a significant amount of water. Japan has a very heavily rice based diet, with sea based protein ingredients, specifically with seafood and aqua cultivation. Japanese science and research teams lead in developing new ways to improve agriculture output across the world (Shin, 2021).

Japan also suffers from devastating earthquakes and tsunamis, one of which resulted in a natural disaster when an earthquake triggered a tsunami that then destroyed the Fukushima nuclear power plant. The one-two punch of the earthquake and tsunami impacted the world economy, as multiple critical manufacturing industries in Japan went off line, and environmental damage in the quake zone and nuclear fallout zone impacted the Japanese people and sent radioactive debris and contamination across a wide swath of the northern hemisphere. Experts label the disaster a "level 7" event, or the worst possible. The Japanese nation has relied upon nuclear power to compensate for the lack of other national power sources, such as fossil fuels. While this reliance creates a "cleaner" environment, the political, social, and economic fallout of the disaster emerged. In some parts of the world, the accident accelerated plans to close nuclear plants. Some environmental groups increased protesting against Japan, merging the accident with anti-whaling protests for Japanese policies of whaling (Shin, 2021).

In all, Japan provides a specific case study which unites STEM and the Humanities into a robust lesson. Students who examine the nation can explore technology, geography, and societal attitudes by examining this island nation.

China and Global Reach

In contrast to Japan, China, by location and by geotechnic activity, has been gifted with a huge number of natural resources. Yet the region has suffered tremendously from the tectonic activity of earthquakes. China has also engaged in massive geomorphing in creating the Three Gorges Dam and creating huge canals across its nation. China also experiences the geographic advantage of large mountains on its western borders and has used these barriers, in combination with the construction of the Great Wall along the north, to try and create a uniform nation (Rossabi, 2021).

Chinese culture, in conjunction with the Confucian and central government of the civil service and imperial throne, stresses conformity and subservience to the central Imperial government. Historically, the Terracotta Army archaeological discovery demonstrates the power and veneration early Chinese cultures expressed for their God like emperor. The sheer coordinating efforts of creating the Terracotta Army indicate a strong central bureaucracy and control over vast resources. Some of these resources were developed with the long overland trade of the Silk Road, a massive super highway of trade starting in the Asian continent and terminating in the Middle East/Byzantine empires along the mediterranean. The Silk Route, following the desert oasis and steppe, created a massive demand for luxury goods in Europe and a thirst for spices that would trigger an age of exploration in the 1400s that marked the rise of European Imperialism (Rossabi, 2021).

The second major area of Chinese strength lies in the exploration of Zheng He and the great armada's voyage to Africa. Chinese exploration sailed west from mainland to Africa and returned with giraffes and a wide range of other resources in the form of tribute for the Middle Kingdom. As Chinese imperial practice began to exploit the rice culture of southern China, the mineral wealth of northern China, and the grand canals along the eastern region of its metros, China became the power of East Asia, influencing the Southeast Asian kingdoms of the Khomer and Korea. The state religion of Confucianism, in conjunction with the calligraphic writing of the empire, created a centralized bureaucracy which spread out into the villages and farmlands of the hinterlands (Rossabi, 2021.

The Mongols became the only real impediment to the Han, or ethnic Chinese empire, as they invaded and conquered a vast region of the Asian steppe, with an empire which spread to the west. Setting up the last major dynasty of China (Qing) based from Manchuria, or the coal rich north eastern region, the Mongols oversaw the last great era of pre-industrialization in China. As technology and the industrial revolution of the western world spread to the Asian subcontinent, the western world fought a number of wars with China, and took over control of "spheres of influence" with the resulting imbalance of trade with China and the forced purchasing of western manufactured goods for raw materials. The tragedy of the imperial greatness of China controlled by the west is best described by the conquest of the harbors and ports on the coast and control of trade from the interior to the wider world. The forced opium wars saw the west literally poisoning the Chinese population with a drug. It was not until the imperialism of Japan during World War II when the west finally was expelled from China. The Chinese were viewed as an ally against the Japanese. Following the Communist takeover in post World War II, China became a great rival of the non-communist nations and fought proxy wars with the United States in Korea and Vietnam (Rossabi, 2021).

The legacy of western Imperialism can be found in the city states of Macau and Hong Kong. These cities are among the most "western" in the region and contain large leisure, trade, and finance industries which had strong ties to their former imperial rulers. As China reasserts its power, it has taken Hong Kong back from British rule and Macau from the Portuguese (Rossabi, 2021).

Today, because of its central location, its vast resources, and wealth, China has made itself a huge rival for the United States in the rare earth minerals trade and the investment in Africa for infrastructure and growth. Chinese interest in the world has resulted in continued conflict in the South China Sea and tensions over the creation of islands in the middle of this region in order to compete with the west. This conflict, over resources, has extended into cyberspace, as the Dragon empire continues to fund computer programming education at a much higher rate than the western world (Rossabi, 2021).

With continued demands for resources from the "Ring of Fire" and the devastating natural catastrophes from earthquakes and tsunamis caused by eruptions, China has a multitude of resources at its disposal, but with significant challenges for its urban and rural populations (Rossabi, 2021).

South Asian Islands

Indonesia, Malaysia, Brunei, and Papua New Guinea are island-based nations in the southern reaches of the *Ring of Fire.* Their nations are some of the largest, most diverse, and most challenged lands in the world. Formed from Volcanic activity and covered with a biodiversity that rivals few areas in the world, set astride the equator, the Southeast Asian Island nations have vast resources, many of which are a direct result of the Ring of Fire. In other news, these nations also have access to the key choke point of world trade: the Straits of Malacca. Brunei, especially, is an oil wealthy nation that exerts influence as an OPEC nation state. Papua, New Guinea is one of the most geologically impacted islands of the Southeast Asian area, with massive uplifts, and isolated valleys. The island nation is rural, with significant fishing and farming (Cotterelle, 2014).

This region, referred to as the East Indies, brought colonial attention due to the spices which the area grew and harvested. The islands are home to some of the largest Islamic communities in the world. The diversity of language and in the more rural regions of religion demonstrated the vastness of these islands and their uniqueness to the world. The volcanic and other tectonic activities caused by the seismic activities have resulted in devastating natural disasters. In 1883, Krakatoa in Indonesia erupted and created a world-wide climate change for that summer. The ash projected into the atmosphere impacted the northern hemisphere and devastated the area surrounding the volcano. In 2004, a major earthquake just off of the Sumantrian island created a massive and devastating tsunami which ravished the tourism regions of the area. The event happened in the middle of the Christmas holiday, when tourists from Europe were in the area. The fishing industry, a mainstay occupation in the region, was dramatically impacted, as equipment was lost, and a number of species were impacted by the mixing of salt and freshwater, in addition to kill created by being swept inland. The island residents were impacted as the coastal zone, often the heaviest settled and urbanized, was inundated, and fresh water sources were rendered brackish (Cotterelle, 2014) .

South America (Moya, 2010)

The fourth region heavily impacted by the Ring of Fire and plate tectonics is the areas on the Pacific coast of South America. From the Galapagos Islands to the highlands of Peru, Chile, and Ecuador which sit astride the Andes Mountains, South America has a number of biomes and unique environments. Home to the "lungs of the earth" in Brazil, the flora and fauna of the Amazon rainforest are some of the most diverse in the world. Plate tectonics produced significant vertical uplift in the Andes Mountains and created large volcanic belts in the region. The massive volcanic and seismic activities indicate quite clearly that the region is still active, and the population is indeed subject to natural disasters (Moya, 2010).

South America is a great example of the impact of the extremes, from the highest desert in the Western Hemisphere, to the deepest lake in the world. The clues surrounding the areas of the Ring of Fire in South America allow understanding of a wide range of information and class-room expectations (Moya, 2010).

By discussing the Mayan, Aztec, and Incan empires, as well as the present nation states, you can examine the Llama transportation system, and how the steep mountains necessitated those areas to develop the communications networks. You can also look with your students on how the beast of burdens, who were not trained horses, exposed the empress, along with germs and steel, to the invaders, who needed to use the conquered peoples as a way to expand their empires (Moya, 2010).

The impact of geography goes further. The area is also home to floating gardens of the region, as the capital city of the Aztec empire ran out of space due to the mountainous terrain of the basin in which they lived. The Incas pioneered terrace farming, or carving flat beds into the sides of large mountains for agricultural purposes. If not erosion after rain was a guarantee. The Mayans demonstrated how to grow cacao and maize and how to fish using spear techniques in an area of massive biodiversity. The area's empires were some of the largest of the world, let alone the western Hemisphere (Moya, 2010).

In South America, the mining and forestry operations for minerals, metals, and arbor based products is widespread, and with oil and gold, lumber and rubber leading as exports, the food export business of tropical fruits and beef have created the infrastructure for wealth, except for interference in political and economic issues by former colonial nations. The Monroe Doctrine and the Roosevelt Corollary facilitated some level of colonization by the United States after the Portuguese, Spanish, French, and English colonial empires began to withdraw as rebellions and European based wars transformed the race from colonization to "protectionism" and the associated economic benefits (Moya, 2010).

Pacific ocean seismics created a number of excellent case studies for teachers in a wide number of classes to examine and explore. The *Ring of Fire*, or Pacific, is one of the largest locations of wealth, and geopolitical rivalry, from the superpowers of the US, Russia, China, and Japan, through the proxy war states of South East Asia, and Korea. The Australian continent, and Hong Kong, Singapore, Macao, and other zones of influence/former colonies have found post World War II economic footing. With the changing tides of economics and manufacturing into "Smart Technologies," the regions in South East Asia and South America have found themselves once again in the spotlight of the world, for natural resources and human capital (Moya, 2010).

Thought Break

How can you utilize the Ring of Fire in your classroom?

8. HEARTS'S NATURAL HABITAT: MUSEUMS

I love museums! I love the past, present, and science of the museums which I have visited. Growing up in Buffalo. New York, there are a ton of museums, including the Turtle Native American Center, the Buffalo Museum of Science, the Buffalo and Erie County Historical Society, Old Fort Niagara, the Buffalo Naval and Service Park, and a number of churches and historic sights around the region (Gradwell & Leacock, 2020).

To the north in Toronto exists a mega metropolis of museums, including the ROM or Royal Ontario Museum, The Ontario Science Center, and a host of others. Museums in cities like Boston, Philadelphia, and Chicago create so many resources for students and teachers. The museums are integral in mixing and matching HEARTS together.

While looking at museums, art galleries, libraries, and historical societies, we have a great set of community resources prepared and ready for teachers, educators, and parents to use. The question is how? Right now we cannot train teachers effectively to teach because of the multitude of demands. Rather, we must ensure that teachers and professionals become linked to work together to create a more nuanced approach to HEARTS. I want to first, however, address a rather large issue that has emerged recently that is beginning to appear in the literature and discourse (Gradwell & Leacock, 2020).

Ethics

With the past being different than today, museum visits need to start with ethics, especially in the areas of acquisition of objects and their display (Miller, 2020). For many museums, the challenges facing their acquisition of objects create some very uncomfortable questions. With the antiquarian movement coinciding with the height of imperialism, many museums acquired objects in their collections through outright theft. Antiquarians in misguided quests went into areas that were under imperial rule and excavated out priceless treasures, cultural heritage artifacts, and human remains. Areas in Africa, Asia, South America, and the United States, specifically native nations, have requested the return of sacred objects, their ancestors' remains, and compensation for desecration of final resting places. Museums have begun to repatriate objects and remains to their descendants and home nations (Miller, 2020).

Ethically speaking, many museums have maintained a practice of displaying animals in taxidermy states, with questionable methods of hunting used to collect those specimens. Many museums are shifting away from accepting donations of animals hunted and rather accepting natural or accidental death. This is especially true of animals protected by endangered status and collaborations with zoos, who have begun to rethink displays for animals (Miller, 2020).

The third major wave of ethical considerations is the treasure hunters of World War II. Often some members of the armies participated in looting, and this has continued into the present day. Whenever war is fought, looting can happen, even if the UN conventions and other documents reveal cultural treasures should not be a target. Especially damaging are the horrid genocides and ethnic cleansing, which have destroyed statuary, cemeteries, museums, archives, and libraries in areas of conflict around the globe. There is an attempt in the 21st century to focus on and reverse the looting and illegal seizure of art and cultural items. Very high profile cases are in the news, as museums find themselves explaining why their collections include pieces stolen from victims of genocide and ethnic conflict (Miller, 2020).

Fourth, ethics have emerged in the ways in which creators of arts and cultural objects are compensated. The art markets, auction houses, and import export markets often see the dealers well remunerated, while artists are starving. In other examples, museums have been questioned vigorously in the areas of deaccession of collections through sales. Many museums are shifting collection goals, and running into financial issues which have been exacerbated by the declining economy and COVID 19 pandemic. In order to keep the museums open, fund much needed repairs, as well as enhance collections to include under-represented artists, many institutions are selling parts of their collections. The media, museum critics, and others have questioned decisions made by governing boards, leadership, and collections specialists (Miller, 2020).

The Science of Museums

For many children and adults, a museum can be a magical place which demonstrates AMAZING interactive exhibits and creative explanations of science, technology, engineering, and math. Exhibits on DNA, and the variety of flora and fauna, coupled with explanations about the five senses, create magic for the whole family and community. When you walk through a museum, you can see dinosaurs, fossils, experimentation, and the static electricity device that raises your mom's hair in the air! You can move to mummies and see pottery created over 3,000 years ago! You may even be able to touch objects in the *YES PLEASE*

TOUCH! children's zones, where you can create music with PVC pipes, or ride a bicycle and generate power (Gradwell & Leacock, 2020).

Exhibits include pulleys, levers, and the physics of fulcrums. You can, with the class, participate in earning badges, and certificates for attending and participating in exhibits. What is even better is the makerspaces which are emerging in many museums, where the organizations are teaching students how to create 3 D print objects, or start a rock collection, or search for a semi-precious gemstone, or look at a telescope and see a comet, or participate in a morse code conversation with a child around the world! (Gradwell & Leacock, 2020)

So why do we not use museums more? Cost, time, and knowledge are the three leading roadblocks to museums and their uses. With the rapid defunding, and shifting prioritization of philanthropy in the US, almost all museums are significantly underfunded, and lack the resources necessary to carry out their missions. Most museums also have to self finance by selling tickets, and this eliminates folks who cannot afford the ticket cost from experiencing the museum's offerings. Acquiring and preserving artifacts are costly as well. In many ways, an old object is a decaying object, and the air conditioning, preservation labs, and display cases are expensive, and require costly and expensive support systems to monitor the quality of the artifacts within the cases (Miller, 2020).

Cost issues also lead to the time issue. Many museums are open during "business hours" as it is a job/career for the employees, many of whom are trying to balance work and life. Second, many museums cannot afford to open in hours outside of the "regular calendar" as the expenses of paying for evening hours or weekend hours can be prohibitive. With the decrease in funding, less time is available for staff to partner with other groups, especially educators, who themselves are often stretched as non-core work has been piled on to our career through the consistent subtraction of support staff and increased digital demands. When museum staff must preserve, fundraise, customer experience, and so many other responsibilities, they do not have time left to do any more work with another group (Gradwell & Leacock, 2020; Miller, 2020).

Expertise is the third area. Many museum staff are trained in areas beyond education, and are working hard to do a lot, but the museums do not have the curriculum expertise required to offer teachers out of the box lessons that align with state and federal standards. These efforts require extensive training and expertise. The efforts are difficult and require extreme amounts of staff time to ensure that the alignment works with the museum, but also for the classroom. We are also seeing, in a very positive development, a demand to hear and see the voices of the underrepresented. This movement, which is righting wrongs, has caused our system to find itself in retraining mode. Far too often in the past, our museum and education programs have failed to take into consideration voices underrepresented, and frankly, ignored by previous collection priorities, and develop displays and curriculum which would inspire and educate a number of generations! (Schero, 2022)

Creating Play and Exploration

As we explore museums, the ethics, the science, and the new social sciences of museums allow for educators and museum experts to refocus their efforts on play. From all of our STEM areas, and our humanities, we know that children love mummies, dinosaurs, and the stars. Children are natural explorers who want to look, touch, listen, and share with their parents and others the joys and wonders of science. Museums are moving away from static exhibits that permit only reading and seeing. So many museums have childrens and discovery centers where the motto "please touch" is prominently displayed. Children can feel the physical sensation of an earthquake or a tornado. The children can handle a fossil. The centers allow for the creation of mummies, or pots, or tools, all through the wonderment of play and creation. Just as experimental archaeology calls for professionals to learn by doing, the museums and the field centers of animals and nature create wonderment, excitement, lifelong memories, and a long lasting belief in science and the ability of people to take in the past and learn something about its rhythms and flows (Gradwell & Leacock, 2020).

Thought Break:

What excites you about going to museums in the past?

*What bothered you about going to museums?

Museums in a Box

Like many resource-starved community and culture organizations, schools, museums, archives, and historical societies have failed to engage in collaboration due to lack of time, resources, and expertise. As I mentioned earlier, there is a lack of time, because everyone is covering so many different responsibilities and jobs! There is a lack of money as the United States does not adequately support museums, and many are forced to rely on fundraising and admissions. Finally, while books are becoming available, there are few schools that intentionally teach how professionals can break across silos and collaborate. Some do try, but are few and far between, and need experts who have time, treasure (usually through grants), and knowledge on whom to reach out to (Mitchell, et al 2019)..

We need to create museums in a box. We must, as a profession, tie the amazing art, science, history, and technology into exploring resources of actual objects for children to use and experiment with in the classroom. We as a profession need to work with our "detritus of the past" and find ways to place non-crucial historical objects into a box and allow students to touch and interact with the past. Often there are so many non-historically significant objects at second hand stores, and this is a good place to start. We need students to see the evolution of everyday life in the clothes, kitchen, tools, and toys of the past and the present. Objects and pictures, documents, and written descriptions only go so far. A three-dimensional model with the ability to interact is best (Mitchell et al., 2019).

We will also see virtual (VR) and augmented (AR) reality products become more common. Now cell phone tours are commonplace, and the technology for VR and AR on cell phones, of which many children and adults have one, will allow for children to see videos, interact with location cards, and hear music from the time period. AR and VR will become more common as we move from standard textbooks to digital media, and as the AR/VR goggles become cheaper and more widely available, and as AR/VR develops, we will see students transported back in time to watch recreations and examine the past as it comes alive. Soon I expect the AR/VR world to include taste and smell. The enveloping of the five senses (sight, taste, hearing, touch and smells) has always been one of the most effective ways of students gaining experiences. The experiential learning of sciences and humanities needs to see experiential archaeology and historical re-enactment become more common for today's digital students (Zollo et al., 2021).

In my career, I have been lucky to work with the Albany Institute of History and Art on two projects. First was the Capital Region in 50 objects, and the second involved the Hudson River School movement. In both cases, the director of education wrote a grant and invited teachers to work with her on the museum displays and artifacts to create pedagogical sound lesson plans and resources. In both instances, this labor of love allowed teachers and students, as well as families, access to information on the web and in person. These creative resources allowed the Capital District and the Hudson River School of Art to find their way into classrooms. It was enlightening to work with some amazing professionals in the museum and in the classroom (Sanger, 2016).

One area that seems to emerge frequently in museum and library planning, however, is a dearth of resources for secondary and college instructors. The museums and libraries are frequently fond of and active in creating for elementary-aged students. This is wonderful, and in no way a negative. Rather it is the lack of materials for older students and their teachers that is often frustrating and difficult to enact good, strategic and imaginative pedagogy! Secondary teachers are often at a loss for creative, hands-on, and experiential lessons due to the strictures of the scope, sequence, and high stakes testing from the neo-liberal reform movements.

The focus on proving that children/students have learned a fact or a process has wrecked our educational system, as accountability has reduced the joy of learning to the burden of proving learning occurred. The American education system has created a very isolationist mind set among folks who want to hold teachers accountable by mandating SO MUCH CONTENT that the use of community organizations, cultural institutions, and outside assistance is sacrificed so that content can be covered within the school walls. For the museums, art, library, and historical societies, the goals and missions can be counter intuitive, where preservation of the past becomes more critical than educating citizens about the past (Lacoe et al., 2020).

Thought Break

How can you create a museum in a box?

In-Person Field Trips vs. Virtual

The debate of our lifetime is virtual versus reality. How can we begin as teachers to examine the best practices of each field trip type? What can we do when budgets are tight and safety has become the overwhelming reason?

I remember as a student traveling to the Genesee Historical Museum to see how life came alive during the mid- to late-1800s and early 1900s. In fourth grade, aligned with the state standards, we spent a few hours at the museum, learning about blacksmithing, tin punching, schools, homes, spinning, weaving, and farming. The sights, smells, touches, and sounds of the farm and the past came alive, with the wood smoke of the fire, and the pungent aroma of the oxen in the field. The hard smoothness of the 1880s school house gave way to the warmth and softness of the wool yarn, as the squeals of the piglets competed with the clanging of the hammer on anvil. There was a sense of difference, and a sense of openness, as my class wandered among the buildings. The highlight was, and I kid you not, the Birch Beer flavored hard candy stick that was part of our admissions packet. We could smell the dutch oven delights of upside down apple cake and taste the woodsy flavor of the parsley root we chewed on at the living history center.

As we returned home to our school, I wanted to stay longer, but alas, school dismissal called. Our lives, regulated by the school bell, brings forth one of the biggest issues with the experiential learning process: we are limited by resources. We are limited by reality. So when we discuss AR/VR, the field trips which exist in cyberspace are not all encompassing, but do provide a taste, or a small chance (Harrington, 2009). For those of us who lived through the 2020 pandemic, we know that virtual became the way that everything existed for a few months at least. We began to see telecommuting on a massive scale, and virtual schooling was the norm for a bit (France et al., 2021).

Museums, galleries, libraries, and historical societies offered children and adults an opportunity to visit. Larger, more prestigious places had virtual presence. Now everyone needs an online experience, or the institution will be left behind. The virtual experience allows the incorporation of sight and sound, while touch, taste and feel are left behind. Yet for many of us, with limited resources, the AR/VR trips allow for visits to overseas sights. A more enhanced version of videos is essentially what VR and AR trips allow for, with the previous technologies limiting people to what the producer directed you to see. You now have options, and with the greater amount of reality caught in VR, you and students can experience ancient tombs and Greek, Roman, and Persian temples. You can see and hear the winds on the Sahara and Serengeti. You can explore the terracotta army and see the top of Mt. Fuji. You can hear the roar of a bengal tiger and the rush of the Monsoon winds. AR and VR are limited substitutes, but necessary until we can properly fund museums and cultural centers and allow all children an opportunity to visit and experience (Zolo et al., 2021).

Thought Break

* Where would you like to virtually travel?

STEM in Museums: Exemplars

The first museum I experienced that really brought home the ideas of a STEM museum is the Chicago museum area—which includes the planetarium, the aquarium, and the Museum of Science and Industry. The number of institutions with the earth science, biology, chemistry, and physics components in the "third city" are amazing! I remember seeing such wonders of a horseshoe crab at the aquarium and a starfish in the touch tank. I remember wondering at the stars at the planetarium, and the travel through to the dark reaches of a black hole. The biggest place of amazement has to be the Science and Industry Museum, with every display from atoms to zebra mussels. Similar to Toronto's museums (the ROM, Science Center, and zoo), the Chicago museums allow for exploration into the biology of the human body, the chemistry of the Great Lakes, the earth science of lake effect snow, and the physics of pulleys and block and tackle.

Seeing, touching, and watching the science behind DNA sequences and observing the perpetual motion weight from the earth's rotation were some of the highlights in my memory nearly thirty years later! These experiences were enhanced by the interactive displays and the please touch philosophy of the Industry and Science Museum, where we could turn gears to see how ratios worked and move water in the pneumatic tubes to demonstrate how simple machines and force of water were greater than my elementary-aged mind could comprehend. The awe of experiencing the fossils and then the enemy warship, all on display, and all with guides, explanations at the ready made me gaze in wonder! As I experienced the crystalline formation of amethyst and the weight of coal and lead, I wanted to know more! I wanted to understand more! I wanted to experience more!

Museums, cultural institutions, and explorations where the student/child can do are so much more inspiring than the old cabinet of curiosities (Lacoe et al., 2020)! How many of us want to enact the fiction books we have read, that by exploring and finding some long lost object, we gain magic, or have an adventure, or experience excitement! If we, as educators, allow our students the opportunity to see, feel, smell, hear, and taste new experiences, we have the student hooked. If we adopt experiential practices, we cannot fail; we can inspire. At museums across the world, not only are virtual experiences waiting, but live, in reality events are just waiting as well.

We should become ready and able to interact with our museum partners in the development and implementation of field trips, experiments, and events. We should, especially where feasible, have children at museums and galleries. We must have folks who do living history, and science, and technology interact with our students! Who doesn't love the Van De Graff generator—and our hair sticking straight up! Who doesn't enjoy the pop and fizz of lithium when it's exposed to the air? What child can resist petting a snake? For centuries, science, history, and technology were discovered not by bookish research, but by collecting, experimenting, and collaborating with others! Going to a museum to see a mummy or dinosaurs, or a bicycle that lights a bulb are events which inspire. We need to realize, as educators, we cannot stand by the limits that the theoretical funding crunch has forced us to accept. We must collaborate and use resources that are in the community, as well as our own classrooms, to create joy and excitement at the prospect of seeing the new and experiencing the amazing!

While museums have a mission to preserve the past, I really hope that many new educators and directors will comb through their collections and create traveling museums and bring those boxes into classrooms, if the children cannot go to the museum. We need students to be intrigued by the past, and by science and technology if we have any hope of reversing the anti-intellectualism, and frankly lack of curiosity, that has run rampant in current American society. We have teachers in rural America, suburban America, and urban America all doing amazing and innovative practices in their classrooms (Lacoe et al.,

2020). They are recreating the discovery of museums and galleries and pressing forward experiential learning. Through herculean tasks, competitive grants, and general stubbornness to not accept the as is, these educators, these professionals need the help and collaboration. While priceless artifacts and one of a kind cannot, nor should not, leave, there are so many other materials and objects that would make exceptional opportunities for students to learn! It's the second and third level, the common, that in abundance should be in circulation. The libraries in Rochester, New York have made so many objects in their collections available. These lending objects include paintings, music, and materials. It works for them, and maybe museums can see to their collections to move out from locked vaults and into the educational systems.

In this past chapter, I explored how museums are a significant collaborative place for STEM. We looked at how HEARTS can come alive at our places of history, science and technology. We looked at the ethical dilemmas many museums are facing and how the practice has grown and evolved. I provided some concrete examples of museums who do well. I also explained how schools and museums should collaborate, and specifically cited the Museum in a box as one way to enact this change!

Thought Break

What is one museum in a box unit you would like to see and why?

CONCLUSION

The preceding chapters were a wild and crazy ride into interdisciplinary work. Being an educator is not easy, and knowing a little about a lot is so mentally draining! As educators, we have been challenged to know, our entire lives in school, the correct or right answer—after all, in the days of yore, schooling was all about knowledge acquisition as a way to sort the managers from the workers. Now, in the 21st Century, the skills we need our teachers and students to know and understand are higher along the "Bloom" pyramid—we need folks who can evaluate and create knowledge (Krathwohl, 2002). We need folks who live at the margins, and intersections of the previously siloed information presented as stand alone content areas. Our civilization depends on people who understand how knowledge is created. We need people to believe in why knowledge is created. We need people to participate in knowledge creation (Nichols, 2017).

In the previous chapters, I focus on how to re-engage and create active citizens through the development of HEARTS. With the world at the end of the 2010s decade, two divergents happened. First, we emphasized science, technology, engineering and math. How we as a western society did this however was clumsy and archaic. We allowed "reformers" to create a series of tests that students needed to pass, and teachers were evaluated by, in order to deem learning was happening. We allowed the accountability movement to destroy the creativity and enjoyment teachers and students had developed in schooling for some. We doubled down on "scientifically based research practices" and forced so much work onto educators that they burned out, and our classrooms and schools were staffed with many novice teachers who were told "scores higher, or your fired" without sufficient time to grow and develop as educators and become knowledgeable about a wide range of information (Ravitch, 2016).

Our higher education institutions also fell victim to the accountability movement, as colleges and universities were suddenly told that the granting of a degree was no longer sufficient to prove learning occurred. Accreditation agencies grew like mushrooms, and demanded fertilizer for compliance and paperwork. We sent colleges and universities along a path of demanding more and saw society cut funding by massive amounts. For many colleges, the budget and resources from previous governmental sources were no longer sufficient, and loans transferred the economic burdens to students and families in debt by tens (if not hundreds) of thousands of dollars. As faculty left or retired, their lines were not replaced, and instead compliance administrators, often underpaid and overworked, were instead hired to keep schools out of litigation. Our liberal arts idea of learning became politicized, as politicians demanded that students have a real applicable skill for the real world, and that areas where a direct one-to-one match was difficult to make were cut in the name of efficiency and effectiveness (Ravitch, 2016).

We are missing folks who understand a wide and broad range of subjects. We are missing the "Renaissance" definition of a citizen: one who is active and knowledgeable in a wide range of subjects (Epstein, 2021; Nichols, 2017). Far too often in the US, there existed an anti-intellectual trend, and it has come home to roost (Merkley, 2020). Throughout this little book, I have tried to show you HOW it is possible to recreate integrative learning through cross-disciplinary units. In my own college methods classes, I ask my students, who are under a year away from being teachers, to cross the disciplinary line, and find the connections across the standards, the frameworks, and the field documents.

In the introduction, I clearly demonstrated that we need to see more anger or rage against where our political antics have led us. I ask for people to take a moment and evaluate if the current is as acceptable as the past. I ask folks to believe that reintegrating STEM and the Arts and Humanities is essential to creating better citizens, students, and communities. I created an argument that children want an enriching curriculum, yet many are not challenged and not supported. We have dampened, structurally, the natural curiosity of kids to ensure they are compliant in a factory school setting. After almost two hundred years, why aren't we teaching better (thank you Dr Larry Cuban (Cuban, 1993)?

In Chapter 1, I discussed the social sciences, and demonstrated how much this one subfield really has to offer to our students, our teachers, and society. From history, political science, economics, anthropology, and geography, our social studies has so many STEM aligned fields that need and want and demand the use of these cross-disciplinary works. I show in the chapter how centering our school system on social studies will actually create better lessons, units, and citizens, as the "squishy" subjects of ethics and community engagement, when tied into stem create a much greater focal point, especially for a generation of passionate students who are demanding reforms in society.

In Chapter 2, I examined the sciences and described the range of interesting and engaging areas of geology, biology, chemistry and physics. I explored how the major sciences are all interconnected, and how the unique areas of expertise can create a steady diet of exploration and analysis. I used chapters 1 and 2 to lay the foundations of the interdisciplinary areas of science, technology, engineering, arts, humanities, and math to create a more engaging and interactive curriculum for all students.

In Chapter 3, I examined the watershed of the Susquhanna to explore how to integrate HEARTS. This major river is a critical area of the Northeast, and the HEARTS content in the chapter provides a model lesson for how any classroom teacher can set up and examine their local waterways as a lesson to engage their learners with local place based content and HEARTS exercises. The chapter is directed at the emerging field of citizen scientists and allows more "civilians" to engage in efforts to save the environment.

In Chapter 4, I explained how professional development is the only way that HEARTS will emerge. The need to help all teachers across all disciplines is necessary, as thinking in cross-disciplinary fashion is cognitively hard, and teaching in a cross disciplinary or interdisciplinary manner requires support. Especially relevant is the need to increase our resources to, and training of teachers who are working with the rising numbers of new English learners and our special needs population. Professional development needed to implement better teaching is so necessary to our schools, and was one of the first areas cut by the last three major economic recession, as resources collapsed.

In Chapter 5, I focused on the gamification movement, and how playing a game can actually spark interest in HEARTS. In providing an interactive game which explores the various areas of HEARTS, students can see and implement decision-making that is low stakes, fun, and interactive as a way of permitting students to see abstract and in many easy arcane ideas come alive. Gamification, which has grown in popularity in recent years, allows students and teachers the ability to engage in learning. Both participant and educator see progress, and allow for student decision-making on what to learn and how fast to learn on a path to flourish.

Gamification also allows students to promote, with pride, through badges, and accomplishments, what they have learned. This trend, in the business world as well, models what the military, scouts, and other recognition systems have promoted: allow students to show what they have learned.

In Chapter 6, my colleague Nancy and I discussed how to use cemetery research as a way to integrate HEARTS. Most villages and towns have a cemetery, and realistically, many children want to know more. Less about death, but about life. A cemetery is the community history written in stone, and the HEARTS possibilities are limitless in the place that is one part memory bank, one part nature preserve, and one part science in real-time. The work of creating an innovative, engaging, and realistic investigation from a cemetery models what we need for students, a greater understanding of their past, and a greater understanding of the future. We can create sacred learning with respect in sacred spaces, beyond the school walls. I am amazingly thankful for Nancy's cooperation, knowledge, and expertise in this chapter!

Chapter 7 explored the Pacific Rim in a time we must be more aware and involved with our neighbors. The Pacific has such rich humanities, social sciences, and technology, and with rising tensions, our students must have an understanding of the HEARTS areas in relation to the Eastern frontier, or the middle kingdom, as China described itself. As educators, we must pay significantly more attention to our non-western cultures, and begin the process of quickly shifting our focus from a Eurocentric approach to a true world civilization approach. It will not be easy, but it is the hard work which must be accomplished if the United States is to remain relevant in the 21st Century and beyond.

The final Chapter, 8, examined a natural institution of HEARTS, the museum world, and the possibilities which emerge when a museum or other institutions are explored, examined, and modeled by teachers and educators. The museums of old, the dusty cabinets of curiosities, are long gone, and our more interactive world of museums are the frontier in how education will be examined for the next century to emerge. As educators seek to do a world full of exploration, utilizing museums will make their lives significantly better, and our students' experiences more enriching. The takeaway from the chapters is simple. Museums have a great potential to create amazing potential.

Throughout the book, you, dear reader, were given an opportunity to participate in thought breaks. Please, look at those thoughts again in one year. If this book is a college assignment, keep it. I believe you will grow as you reflect during your own professional journey. I once told my Methods of Social Studies undergraduates, what the professors do is a disservice. You CANNOT survive without integrating all of the subjects (Rhodes, et al, 2022). Siloed curriculum, testing in only federally mandated areas, and public "report cards" on schools changed our profession. Burnout in 2023 is at an all time high among teachers. School violence is a national emergency. Teachers are, as a profession, called to task without the resources needed. The nation must do better. YOU CAN NOT DO THIS ALONE! Mental health matters- if you feel overwhelmed or need help, please get it! YOU ARE TOO VALUABLE AS A HUMAN TO LOSE! A job is just that. Teaching IS A JOB! NOTHING MORE! Take breaks, limit what you do for a system. Your students will be okay- because you care. That is plenty.

I wish to end with one simple thought in my conclusion. I cannot believe that in my professional career so much has changed. So many folkways in teaching have gone extinct, like the dodo bird. These shared experiences of field trips, museums, and hands-on learning were ruthlessly hunted by so-called reformers. Many of these change agents were not teachers, nor experts on anything but change. I am however, extremely hopeful, and buoyed by the efforts I see in my methods classes, and in the field. I see so many fighting the battle against boring instruction and test-based learning. I see so many teachers demanding folks who do not know better get out of their way, so that learning and growth can flourish. I see classrooms where learning is the priority. I see classrooms where experimentation is the order of the day. I see creativity in chaos, and exclamations of joy, wonder, and disappointment when the time runs out, because the students want to experience and learn. I see so many teachers giving heroic efforts in the face of bureaucratic opposition and demands for accountability measuring what matters to reformers, not to the students and their communities.

I hear, I see, I feel, and I proclaim your wonder, your effort, and your strength!

Impostor Syndrome whispered, "you are not good enough" and we, oh we few screamed back, "enough, for we are great!"

BIBLIOGRAPHY

Agulair, E. (2014). 10 Tips for delivering awesome professional development. *Edutopia.* Downloaded: https://www.edutopia.org/blog/10-tips-delivering-awesome-professional-development-elena-aguilar

Ashton, J. (2014). Beneath the veneer: Marginalization and exclusion in an inclusive co-teaching context. *International Journal of Whole Schooling 10*(1), 43-62.

Ballantine, J. H., Hammack, F. M., & Stuber, J. (2017). *The sociology of education: A systematic analysis.* Routledge.

Barab, S., et al (2012). Game-based curriculum and transformational play. *Computers & Education,* 58, 518-533.

Benedict, A. et al. (2014). Taking charge of your professional learning. *Teaching Exceptional Children 46(6),* 147-157.

Benjamin, D. & Komolos, D. (2021). Working Parents Are Exhausted And About To Jump Ship. Here's How Leaders Can Retain Them With Work parent-Friendly Practices. Forbes: https://www.forbes.com/sites/benjaminkomlos/2021/05/25/working-parents-are-exhausted-and-about-to-jump-ship-heres-how-leaders-can-retain-them-with-workparent-friendly-practices/?sh=1bed4d5c4c1b

Berg, W. (2010). *Local newspapers, drinking water pathways, and dimensions of knowledge: Public awareness amid the hydrofracking debate.* State University of New York College of Environmental Science and Forestry.

Bonacchi, C. (2013). Audiences and experiential values of archaeological television: The case study of time team. *Public Archaeology, 12*(2), 117-131.

Bonner, F., & Jacobs, J. (2017). The persistence of television: The case of The Good Life. *Critical Studies in Television, 12*(1), 6-20.

Borek, J. (2008). A nation at risk at 25. *Phi Delta Kappan, 89*(8), 572-574.

Boyle, E. (2016). An update to the systematic literature review of empirical evidence of the impacts and outcomes of computer games and serious games. *Computers & Education*, 94, 178-192.

Brown, M., Rodríguez, N. N., & Updegraff, A. (2023). We need a curricular cooperative: envisioning a future beyond teachers paying teachers. *Learning, Media and Technology*, 1-14.

Bruggerman, J. (2023). Down and out at the AHA. *Chronicle of Higher Education.* Downloaded: https://www.chronicle.com/article/down-and-out-at-the-aha

Callahan, C., Saye, J., & Brush, T. (2016). Interactive and collaborative professional development for in-service history teachers. *The Social Studies, 107*(6), 227-243.

Carr, P. &M. Kefalas (2009). *Hollowing Out The Middle.* Boston: Beacon.

Cervone, J. A. (2017). *Corporatizing rural education: Neoliberal globalization and reaction in the United States.* Springer.

Cotterell, A. (2014). *A history of South East Asia.* Marshall Cavendish International Asia Pte Ltd.

Cramer, K. (2016) *Politics of rage.* Chicago, IL: University of Chicago Press.

Cuban, L. (1993). *How teachers taught: Constancy and change in American classrooms, 1890-1990.* Teachers College Press.

Darling-Hammond, L., Bae, S., Cook-Harvey, C. M., Lam, L., Mercer, C., Podolsky, A., & Stosich, E. L. (2016). Pathways to new accountability through the Every Student Succeeds Act. *Palo Alto, CA: Learning Policy Institute.*

De Blij, H. J., Muller, P. O., & Nijman, J. (1997). *Geography: realms, regions, and concepts.* Wiley.

De La Paz, S., Monte-Sano, C., Felton, M., Croninger, R., Jackson, C., & Piantedosi, K. W. (2017). A historical writing apprenticeship for adolescents: Integrating disciplinary learning with cognitive strategies. *Reading Research Quarterly, 52*(1), 31-52.

Dickens, C. (2004). *The annotated christmas carol: A Christmas Carol in Prose.* WW Norton & Company.

Delisle, J. R. (2021). *Dumbing down America: The war on our nation's brightest young minds (and what we can do to fight back).* Routledge.

DuFour, R. (2014). Harnessing the power of PLCs. *Educational Leadership, 71*(8), 30-35.

Duncan, G. J., & Murnane, R. J. (Eds.). (2011). *Whither opportunity?: Rising inequality, schools, and children's life chances.* Russell Sage Foundation.

Edweek (2021). Where Critical Race Theory is under attack. Downloaded from: https://www.edweek.org/policy-politics/map-where-critical-race-theory-is-under-attack/ 2021/06

Ellis, C., Adams, T. E., & Bochner, A. P. (2011). Autoethnography: an overview. *Historical social research/Historische sozialforschung,* 273-290.

Epstein, D. (2021). *Range: Why generalists triumph in a specialized world.* Penguin.

Erduran, S. (2020). Science education in the era of a pandemic. *Science & Education, 29*(2), 233-235.

France, D., Lee, R., Maclachlan, J., & McPhee, S. R. (2021). Should you be using mobile technologies in teaching? Applying a pedagogical framework. *Journal of Geography in Higher Education, 45*(2), 221-237.

Gee, J. P. (2014). *Collected essays on learning and assessment in the digital world.* Urbana-Champaign, IL: Common Ground Publishing.

Gerwin, D. (2014). What lies Beyond the Bubble? Trying out one of the Stanford History Education Group's new history assessments. *The Social Studies, 105*(6), 266-273.

Giraldez, A. (2001). A review of a world that trade created. *Journal of World History 12*(2), 482-485.

Gjicali, K., & Lipnevich, A. A. (2021). Got math attitude?(In) direct effects of student mathematics attitudes on intentions, behavioral engagement, and mathematics performance in the US PISA. *Contemporary Educational Psychology, 67*, 102019.

Gore, J., & Rosser, B. (2022). Beyond content-focused professional development: powerful professional learning through genuine learning communities across grades and subjects. *Professional development in education, 48*(2), 218-232.

Gradwell, J. M., & Leacock, K. H. (2020). *Finding history where you least expect it.* American Museum Alliance.

Granger, J. (2020). The Literary Alchemy of JK Rowling. In A. Mammary (Ed), *The Alchemical Harry Potter: Essays on Transfiguration in JK Rowling's Novels* (pp. 30-45). McFarland.

Grant, S. G. (2013). Inquiry, instruction, and the potential of the College, Career, and Civic Life (C3) Framework. *Social Education, 77*(6), 322-326, 331.

Grant, S. G., Swan, K., & Lee, J. (2015). Bringing the C3 framework to life. *Social Education, 79*(6), 310-315.

Guiley, R. (2001). *The encyclopedia of saints.* Infobase Publishing.

Hamari, J. et al. (2016) Challenging games help students learn. *Computers in Human Behavior,* 54, 170-179.

Harrington, M. C. (2009). An ethnographic comparison of real and virtual reality field trips to Trillium Trail: the salamander find as a salient event. *Children Youth and Environments, 19*(1), 74-101.

Harrison, R. L., & Parks, B. (2017). How STEM can gain some STEAM: Crafting meaningful collaborations between STEM disciplines and inquiry-based writing programs. In *Writing Program and Writing Center Collaborations* (pp. 117-139). Palgrave Macmillan US.

Hess, A. (2019). 24% of Americans haven't read a book in the past year. *CNBC.* Downloaded: *https://www.cnbc.com/2019/01/29/24-percent-of-american-adults-havent-read-a-book-in-the-past-year--heres-why-.html*

Ho, L., McAvoy, P., Hess, D., & Gibbs, B. (2017). Teaching and learning about controversial issues and topics in the social studies. *The Wiley handbook of social studies research,* 319-335.

Hofstadter, R. (1963). *Anti-intellectualism in American Life*. Vintage.

Holzner, S., & Wohns, D. F. (2015). *U can: Physics for dummies*. John Wiley & Sons.

Jakubowski, C. (2021). *A Cog in the Machine*. Edumatch.

Jakubowski, C. (2020). Thinking about teaching. Edumatch.

Jakubowski, C. (2019). Hidden Resistance. Unpublished PhD Diss. SUNY Albany, NY.

Jans, M. (2004). Children as citizens: Towards a contemporary notion of child participation. *Childhood, 11*(1), 27-44.

Jones, C. F. (2014). *Routes of power*. Harvard University Press.

Kelly, S. & Nardi B. (2014). Playing sustainability: Using video games to simulate futures of scarcity. *First Monday, 19*:5.

Kimmerle, J. et al. (2015). Learning and collective knowledge with social media. *Educational Psychologist, 50*(2), 120-137.

Kohler, P. (2010). Don't just tell me; show me: Using graphic organizers effectively. *Teaching Professor 23*(6), 1-7.

Kramer, A. M. (2011). Mediatizing memory: History, affect and identity in who do you think you are?. *European Journal of Cultural Studies, 14*(4), 428-445.

Krathwohl, D. R. (2002). A revision of Bloom's taxonomy: An overview. *Theory into Practice, 41*(4), 212-218.

Kratz, R. F. (2017). *Biology for dummies*. John Wiley & Sons.

Labaree, D. F. (1996). The trouble with ed schools. *The Journal of Educational Foundations, 10*(3), 27.

Lacoe, J., Painter, G. D., & Williams, D. (2020). Museums as classrooms: The academic and behavioral impacts of "School in the Park". *AERA Open, 6*(3), 2332858420940309.

Langreo, L (2023). 5 big challenges for schools in 2023. EdWeek: https://www.ed-week.org/leadership/5-big-challenges-for-schools-in-2023/2023/01

Lesh, B. A. (2011). *Why won't you just tell us the answer: Teaching historical thinking in grades 7-12*. Stenhouse Publishers

Littenberg-Tobias, J. (2021). Teaching citizens: What can NAEP civics tell us about active learning in civics?. *Peabody Journal of Education, 96*(3), 247-260.

Lowell, B. R., Cherbow, K., & McNeill, K. L. (2021). Redesign or relabel? How a commercial curriculum and its implementation oversimplify key features of the NGSS. *Science Education, 105*(1), 5-32.

Lowenthal, D. (1998). *The heritage crusade and the spoils of history*. Cambridge University Press.

MacMath, S., Sivia, A., & Britton, V. (2017). Teacher perceptions of project based learning in the secondary classroom. *Alberta Journal of Educational Research, 63*(2), 175-192.

Maguth, B., et al. (2015). Teaching social studies with video games. *The Social Studies, 106* (1), 32-36.

McHenry-Sorber, E. (2014). The power of competing narratives: A new interpretation of rural school-community relations. *Peabody Journal of Education, 89*(5), 580-592.

Merkley, E. (2020). Anti-intellectualism, populism, and motivated resistance to expert consensus. *Public Opinion Quarterly, 84*(1), 24-48.

Meuwissen, K. W. (2017). "Happy professional development at an unhappy time": Learning to teach for historical thinking in a high-pressure accountability context. *Theory & Research in Social Education, 45*(2), 248-285.

Miller, S. (2020). *Museum Collection Ethics*. London: Rowman & Littlefield.

Miller, D. S., & Rivera, J. D. (2006). Hallowed ground, place, and culture: The cemetery and the creation of place. *Space and Culture, 9*(4), 334-350.

Mitchell, A., Linn, S., & Yoshida, H. (2019). A tale of technology and collaboration: Preparing for 21st-century museum visitors. *Journal of Museum Education, 44*(3), 242-252.

Moe, T. M. (2011). *Special interest: Teachers unions and America's public schools.* Brookings Institution Press.

Molyneux, L. et al. (2015). Gaming social capital: Exploring civic value in multiplayer video games. *Journal of Computer-Mediated Communication* 20, 381-399.

Monmonier, M. (2018). *How to lie with maps.* 3rd edition. University of Chicago Press.

Monroe-Baillargeon, A. & Shema, A.. (2010). Time to talk: An urban school's use of literature circles to create a professional learning community. *Education and Urban Society 42(6),* 651-673.

Moore, J. T. (2019). *Chemistry essentials for dummies.* John Wiley & Sons.

Moya, J. C. (Ed.). (2010). *The Oxford handbook of Latin American history.* Oxford University Press.

Mullgardt, B. (2014). Gaming the Gilded Age. *The Councilor: A Journal of the Social Studies,* 75(1)

Murphy, et al. (2021). Coronia virus deaths. *NBC News: https://www.nbcnews.com/health/health-news/coronavirus-deaths-united-states-each-day-2020-n1177936*

Musser, K. (2007). Susquehanna River Basin. Downloaded: https://commons.wikimedia.org/wiki/File:Susquehanna_River_watershed_map_with_lower_Susquehanna_River_watershed_highlighted.png

NCSS. (2013). *The college, career, and civic life (C3) framework for social studies state standards: Guidance for enhancing the rigor of K-12 civics, economics, geography, and history.* Silver Spring, MD: NCSS.

Newton, M. (2022). *Ancestor trouble.* New York: Random House.

Nichols, T. (2017). *The death of expertise: The campaign against established knowledge and why it matters.* Oxford University Press.

Nokes, J. D. (2017). Historical reading and writing in secondary school classrooms. In *Palgrave Handbook of Research in Historical Culture and Education* (pp. 553-571). Palgrave Macmillan UK.

Oakes, J. (2005). *Keeping track: How schools structure inequality.* Yale University Press.

Ocejo, R. E. (2017). *Masters of craft.* Princeton University Press.

Park, A., & Glascock, J. L. (2010). The performance impact of strategic corporate real estate in franchise organizations. *Journal of Corporate Real Estate.*

Petersen, A. (2016). Perspectives of special education teachers on general education curriculum access: Preliminary results. *Research and Practice for Persons with Severe Disabilities, 41*(1), 19-35.

Pomeranz, K. & Topik, S. (2012). *The world that trade created: Society, culture, and the world economy, 1400 to the present* 3rd ed. Armonk, NY: M. E. Sharpe.

Rabinow, L. (2019). *Persistent: Why New York State and the United States still don't regulate PFOA in drinking water.* Rensselaer Polytechnic Institute.

Ravitch, D. (2016). *The death and life of the great American school system: How testing and choice are undermining education.* Basic Books.

Reich, G. & Bailly, D.. (2010). Get smart: facing high stakes testing together. *The Social Studies 10,.* 179-184.

Reich, G.A.(2011).Testing collective memory: Representing the Soviet Union on multiple-choice questions. *Journal of Curriculum Studies,43*(4),507-532.

Reisman, A. (2017). Integrating content and literacy in social studies: Assessing instructional materials and student work from a common core-aligned intervention. *Theory & Research in Social Education, 45*(4), 517-554.

Resor, C. (2008) Encouraging students to read the text: The jigsaw method. *Teaching History: A Journal of Methods 33(1), 20-27.*

Rhodes, M., et al. (2022). *Crush it from the start: 50 tips for new teachers.* SchoolRubric. 50teachertips.com

Rice, D. & Zigmond, N. (2000). Co-teaching in secondary schools. *Learning Disabilities Research and Practice 15(4)*, 190-197.

Richter, D. K. (2005). *Native Americans' Pennsylvania.* Pennsylvania Historical Association.

Robeyns, I. (2006). Three models of education: Rights, capabilities and human capital. *Theory and research in education*, *4*(1), 69-84.

Rossabi, M. (2021). *A history of China.* John Wiley & Sons.

Rousmaniere, K. (2013). Those who can't, teach: the disabling history of American educators. *History of Education Quarterly*, *53*(1), 90-103.

Rutkowski, D. (2015). The OECD and the local: PISA-based test for schools in the USA. *Discourse: Studies in the cultural politics of education*, *36*(5), 683-699.

Sanger, E (2016). Teacher's material for the Capital District in 50 Objects. Albany Institute of History and Art. Downloaded: https://www.albanyinstitute.org/id-50-objects.html

Schero, J. (2022). Docents and museum education: The past, present, and future. In *Research Anthology on Citizen Engagement and Activism for Social Change* (pp. 74-103). IGI Global.

Scribner, C. F. (2016). *The fight for local control.* Cornell University Press.

Shaw, R. E. (2014). *Canals for a nation: The canal era in the United States, 1790-1860.* University Press of Kentucky.

Shelton, C. C., Koehler, M. J., Greenhalgh, S. P., & Carpenter, J. P. (2022). Lifting the veil on TeachersPayTeachers. com: An investigation of educational marketplace offerings and downloads. *Learning, Media and Technology*, *47*(2), 268-287.

Sherman, J. (2021). *Dividing Paradise.* California University Press.

Shin, K. (2021). The teaching of Asian history as a section of the world history curriculum: The case of American high school teachers. *Asia Pacific Journal of Education*, 1-13.

Siemaszko, C. (2010). Leaders of Sidney, tiny upstate town, demand Muslims dig up bodies at cemetery on land they own. *New York Daily news*. Downloaded from: https://www.nydailynews.com/news/national/leaders-sidney-tiny-upstate-town-demand-muslims-dig-bodies-cemetery-land-article-1.441191

Sipple, J. W., & Yao, Y. (2015). The unequal impact of the great recession on the instructional capacity of rural schools. In Williams & Grooms (Eds), *Educational opportunity in rural contexts: The politics of place* (39-58). Information Age Publishing.

Somerville, A. A., & McDonald, R. A. (2013). *The Vikings and their age*. University of Toronto Press.

Spooner, A. M. (2012). *Environmental science for dummies*. John Wiley & Sons.

Squire, K., & Jenkins, H. (2004). Harnessing the power of games in education. *Insight, 3*, 5-33.

Swan, K., Grant, S. G., & Lee, J. (2012). College, career and civic life (C3): The framework for the state standards for social studies. In *Annual Meeting of the College and University Faculty Assembly, Seattle, WA*.

Thacker, E. (2017). "PD is where teachers are learning!" high school social studies teachers' formal and informal professional learning." *Journal of Social Science Research 41*, 37-52.

Towrek, H. (2013). The real reason the humanities are in crisis. *The Atlantic*. Accessed: https://www.theatlantic.com/education/archive/2013/12/the-real-reason-the-humanities-are-in-crisis/282441/

Tyack, D. B., & Cuban, L. (1995). *Tinkering toward utopia: A century of public school reform*. Harvard University Press.

Walkowiak, T. A., Minogue, J., Harrington, A. D., & Edgington, C. P. (2017). Re-envisioning the school day: Integrating mathematics, science, and reading through students' engagement with practices. *Journal of Interdisciplinary Teacher Leadership, 1*(2), 7-12.

Wallace, P. W. (1961). *Indians in Pennsylvania*. DIANE Publishing Inc.

Walstad, W. B. (2001). Economic education in US high schools. *Journal of Economic Perspectives, 15*(3), 195-210.

Waring, S. M. (2011). *Preserving history: The construction of history in the K16 classroom.* IAP.

Wells, C., Cramer, K. J., Wagner, M. W., Alvarez, G., Friedland, L. A., Shah, D. V., ... & Franklin, C. (2017). When we stop talking politics: The maintenance and closing of conversation in contentious times. *Journal of Communication, 67*(1), 131-157.

Whitson, M. (2021). Attention platform 9¾: The Hogwarts Express is canceled. Exploration in cancel culture, JK Rowling, and beyond. Honors Thesis. Ouachita Baptist University. Downloaded: https://scholarlycommons.obu.edu/cgi/viewcontent.cgi?article=1803&context=honors_theses

Wineburg, S. (2010). Historical thinking and other unnatural acts. *Phi Delta Kappan, 92*(4), 81-94.

Wood, L., Kiperman, S., Esch, R. C., Leroux, A. J., & Truscott, S. D. (2017). Predicting dropout using student-and school-level factors: An ecological perspective. *School Psychology Quarterly, 32*(1), 35.

Zollo, L., Rialti, R., Marrucci, A., & Ciappei, C. (2021). How do museums foster loyalty in tech-savvy visitors? The role of social media and digital experience. *Current Issues in Tourism*, 1-18.

Zukas, A. (2000). Active learning, world history and the internet: Creating knowledge in the classroom. *International Journal of Social Education 15*(1), *62-79.*

Made in the USA
Middletown, DE
02 June 2023

31589825R00096